THROUGH THE STORM

Copyright © Lakeisha McQuinn 2017
All rights reserved.

ISBN: 978-0-692-98409-3

First published by STRATEGIC PURPOSE PRESS
November 2017
www.getthroughthestorm.com

Cover photo by solarseven / 123RF Stock Photo
Book design by Adam Robinson for Good Book Developers

This is a true story, told to the best of the author's memory.

THROUGH THE STORM

AMINA ISRAEL

CONTENTS

xi / Acknowledgments

Chapter 1
1 / Woodcroft

Chapter 2
8 / New Home, New Family

Chapter 3
20 / Turn of Events

Chapter 4
26 / Richmond's Southside

Chapter 5
36 / New Beginnings: Hustling and Motherhood

Chapter 6
47 / Goodbye to Jay

Chapter 7
53 / New York Stints

Chapter 8
62 / Full-Time in the Game at Ruffin Road

Chapter 9
78 / "Boy" and "Girl"

Chapter 10
95   /   Long-Awaited Encounter

Chapter 11
107   /   Betrayal

Chapter 12
124   /   A New Low

Chapter 13
131   /   A Different Hustle

Chapter 14
153   /   Turning Point

Chapter 15
171   /   A New Dawn

Chapter 16
179   /   Finding and Ripping Out the Roots of Ugliness

Chapter 17
191   /   The Other Side of the Storm

198   /   Epilogue

201   /   About the Author

For gold is tried in the fire, and acceptable
men in the furnace of adversity.
— Ecclesiasticus 2:5

To those who struggle—in the present or past.

ACKNOWLEDGMENTS

First and foremost, I'd like to give all praises to the Most High God for making this book possible and for the incredible gift of resilience He has given me. Were it not for His mercy and grace, I don't know where I'd be today. I am humbled by the experiences He brought me through, which culminated in this book.

I also like to thank Bishop Nathanyel, who has been mightily used by the Most High in the spreading of His word. His humility and meekness exemplify how we ought to conduct ourselves as men and women of God (Sirach 21:13, Apocrypha).

I thank also my editor, Mrs. Sabrina, for her adept editorial skills in refining the manuscript so that it tells my story more effectively than it did in its raw form.

Lastly, I thank all three of my children for their support and encouragement during the writing of this book, especially my daughter, who has shown me amazing patience as I poured my heart and time into this book.

They say that after every storm there's a rainbow. Here's mine, but it hadn't always been this way…

CHAPTER 1

WOODCROFT

It was the beginning of the summer days in 1978 when she decided: "Today is the day I make my move."

She stuffed her baby's diaper bag with as much as she possibly could. After wrapping her baby in a blanket to shield her from the drizzles, she headed for the living room with her baby in one arm and the bag in the other. Her three younger siblings were already in the living room, and she kissed them goodbye before darting out the door. Her parents came to the door and screamed after her as she ran away as fast she could, with her eight-month-old baby secure in her arms. Steadily and swiftly she ran, checking her trail every now and then to make sure no one was on her heels. She was tired of suffering at the hands of her abusive stepdad.

She reached the bus stop just as the city bus was pulling in. It stopped directly in front of her and opened its doors. Relieved that she was now at a safe distance away from home, she got on the bus, grabbed the closest seat, and began scoping her surroundings. "What do I do now?" she thought, as she gently adjusted the blanket to reveal her baby's face. She looked at her adoringly, as she continued to think about her next steps.

Two hours and three complete bus routes later, Ms. Jay finally decided where she and her baby would go.

As the day drew to an end in the dusk, Ms. Jay showed up at her grandmother's doorsteps unannounced, with her baby in her arms and nowhere else to turn to. She knocked a few times, expectant of a familiar refuge.

"Who is it?" an older lady asked from the other side of the door.

"It's Jay, Grandma."

Opening the door, the old lady immediately noticed the troubled look in her granddaughter's eyes. "Everything's alright," she said to Jay, taking the baby from her arms and signaled the young woman to follow her in. "If I had known you and Lilbit here were coming, I would've fixed you both some supper."

Now in the living room they both sat. Despite the circumstances, Jay was immediately comforted by the familiar surroundings. An oversized rug hung on wall opposite the couch, embroidered with the likeness of John F. Kennedy, Dr. Martin Luther King, Jr., and Robert Kennedy. A few feet away from the coffee table was the faithful record player that had accompanied Jay's grandmother in more years than Jay could remember.

Jay's grandmother sat down in her favorite rocking chair, playing with the baby's tiny, eager fingers. The distressed Jay exhaled and began. "I ran away from home."

"You what?" Her grandmother looked up at Jay and exclaimed.

"I ran away from home," Jay repeated.

"How could you do such a foolish thing, girl! What on God's green earth would prompt you to do such a thing?"

Jay let her tears loose, not for running away, but because of what she and her siblings had been enduring. "Ma's husband, I can't take it no more." She sobbed as she filled her grandmother's ears with what had been known by no one until that moment. "He's an alcoholic, and when he gets drunk he beats her," she ranted through the tears. "After Mom let him put my brother out of the house, things just got worse." Jay continued about how her brother was only thirteen and already homeless. He was sleeping wherever he could because he wasn't allowed to come back home. That wasn't it. Jay and her siblings were also being fondled and touched by the stepdad in ways that no adult should touch a child. He'd also chain the refrigerator, restricting the children's access to food until he was home and gave them permission. Even when Jay was younger, she was functionally treated as a slave. She cooked, cleaned, washed everybody's clothes, and tended to her siblings, only a few years younger than herself, as if they were her own children.

"I told Ma," Jay said to her grandmother, "but she wouldn't believe me." In fact, when Jay told her mother about his violation and mistreatment of them while she was working or sometimes even at home, she would hear none of it. Seeing that the abuse wouldn't let up, Jay had to do what she deemed necessary for her and her baby. "Grandma, I'm not ever going back there, ever. I don't know where Keisha and I would go if we can't stay here, but there's no way I'm going back to that house."

Her grandmother understood the indirect question and implicit plea, and she decided to lend her granddaughter a helping hand. "Your mother ought to be ashamed of herself. I had no idea those things were going on over there, but it all makes sense now," she said, looking as if she had something on her mind. "Look, you and Lilbit can stay here. You know the place is full but I don't mind if y'all stay." Jay didn't mind. She knew her grandmother's hearth already sheltered many of their large family, but that was why it felt like home.

The older lady stood up, with her great-granddaughter still in her arms, and walked down the hallway. Ms. Jay followed. Reaching the first door on their left, Jay's grandmother opened it to show Ms. Jay her new shared bedroom and handed her back the baby. "I don't care how long y'all stay," she said, "but you need to get a job and help with food and bills, and I'll watch Lilbit when you do that. You keep this room as well as this place clean, you got it?" She then gestured to the hall closet to show Jay where she could find the linen. She kissed both her granddaughter and great-granddaughter on their foreheads and left them to settle down, retreating into her own bedroom.

Now alone with her baby, Jay breathed a sigh of relief, exhausted from the day's events. "Thank you, God, for Grandma, and giving me and my baby a place to stay," Jay said quietly, looking up toward the ceiling. Then the weight of her situation caught her unawares, as she felt her baby heavy in her arms. "Girl, you heavy!" She looked down into the baby's eyes and kissed her. "I'm hungry. Let's see what Grandma's got in here."

Jay walked into the kitchen and opened the refrigerator door after sitting the baby down on the kitchen table. As she looked through the refrigerator, one of her aunts walked through the front door.

"Hey girl, where did you come from?" She approached Jay and hugged her. Before they exchanged greetings, she noticed her great-niece Keisha sitting compliantly on the table. "Oh, look at you!" She walked over and picked up Keisha as Jay began to fill her in on what had happened.

Jay's aunt was only three years her senior, and they had always been close. They talked the night away as long-time confidantes. As their conversation progressed into the night, other members of the family who lived with Jay's grandmother returned and filled the house.

For reasons unknown to me, everyone, including her own children, called my great-grandmother "Sister." She had fourteen children, including two sets of twins. "Sister" was a little lady, standing only four feet and five inches, with a tiny frame. Even as a great-grandmother, her hair was long, jet black, and beautiful. She wore tiny little glasses, which often sat on her nose as she talked casually at length with her large family. As she was the soul of the family, so was her place, a spacious four-bedroom apartment, the center of activity. Relatives came and went, revolving around Sister's home, the anchor of their lives. Her apartment was in the complex "Woodcroft," located at the bottom of the Fulton neighborhood on the east side of Richmond, Virginia.

So there in The Woodcroft Jay settled down with her baby. Before long, I was two and Ms. Jay had given birth to another baby. He was a fat one, and Mom named him Chris. My dad would come and get me sometimes and take me to his mother's house on the weekends. I knew both sides of my family, but Chris's dad was never around. Ms. Jay was the best, though. Chris and I had everything we needed. Sister was known for nicknaming all of her grandchildren and great-grandchildren. She called my brother Biggs. It was probably because he was fat and greedy. Biggs was my favorite of all my playmates. I felt closer to him than to anyone else, maybe because we shared the same mom. Whatever the reason, I loved him and he was extra special to me.

That natural bond with Chris was nurtured at The Woodcroft in the company of our large extended family. Around Sister's house, family time was everything. We and our extended family frequently gathered for dinners for no special purpose; family itself was occasion enough. But Thanksgiving was different—the meals were more elaborate, and the party was larger and lasted longer. Almost always, cold winter snow fell silently outside or was already thick on the ground, when some of the grown-ups rolled up their sleeves in a joint effort in preparing the feast while the others busied themselves catching up with each other. The smell of pine filled the air and Michael Jackson's "Don't Stop 'Til You Get Enough" played over an old boom box and animated the holiday spirits all the more of the relatives that packed Sister's place.

As the dinner preparation was underway, some of the adults entertained in the living room, where Mom gave informal performances. Tina Marie's voice reverberated loudly through the sound system, as Mom sang along into a hairbrush pretending it was her mic. She had a beautiful voice. Even when other kids were playing in a different room, I'd run over to the living room when I heard her voice. I'd sit at her feet, listening to her and imagining her on stage in a spotlight. Everything else would be dark; it would be only Mom and me. Although she'd certainly have a huge audience, but I would be her biggest fan. She was bold, and so was her voice.

After Mom's performance, we'd all join in and, as an odd family tradition, sing Christmas carols on Thanksgiving. Among other things we did at these gatherings, the kids—more precisely, brother, our cousin Smithboy, and I—would be grilled for Bible questions. Throughout the year Sister would make us younger children study Bible questions, I guess in preparation for these occasions. It was always at Thanksgiving and Christmas that she put us in front of the family and then grilled us on our catechism. The three of us stood in the middle of the living room, with music off and all eyes on us, and she'd begin.

"Who made you?"

"God."

"What else did God make?"

"All things," we'd say in unison.

"Why did He make you and all things?"

"To glorify His name."

"What were the three steps to Jacob's ladder"?

"The Father, the Son, and—" before all three of us completed our response in one accord, Smithboy blurted out, "—and the billy goat! Yep, the billy goat."

I think the five-year-old Smithboy had gotten tired of the same repetitive patterns and decided to give a little humor.

The entire family roared in laughter. Seeing that Smithboy failed to give the correct answer in the solemn manner expected of him, which should have ended in "the Holy Ghost," Sister continued with her thousand questions. When the questioning ended, after what seemed like a million years, we ran off to join the other kids, who were curiously left out of the ordeal we had to endure, and continued playing and laughing.

Finally, the much-anticipated announcement came. "Dinner's ready!" At that, we kids stumbled past one another like a herd of wild animals in our race to get to the table. The large dining table, which drew relatives from all corners of the home to sit down together and partake of the same meal, would have a bright orange cloth draped over it and weird-shaped objects set in the middle of it—weird to me, anyway. I still can't recall what they were or were supposed to represent.

Before dinner was served, all of us, adults and children, formed a giant circle around the table. With joined hands, we all bowed our heads as Sister led the prayer giving thanks to God. We would then take our seats, quietly and courteously, as if our good behavior would hasten the service of the food.

In between hearty bites of the usual Thanksgiving dishes, the grown-ups talked and laughed and joked, clinking their tall glasses that had red juice in them. We, the wee ones, always got some juice of a different color. We weren't allowed to have the same juice as the adults. It didn't matter to us, though, because sugar was sugar.

A less strange family tradition at Thanksgiving (compared to singing Christmas carols on Thanksgiving Day) was setting up and decorating the Christmas tree after the Thanksgiving dinner. This was the third best part of the evening for me, after the eating and the playing. As dozens of people all put their hands into the tree decoration, the living room buzzed with energy and warmth. Sister would grab one of her many black Frisbees—which I later learned were her prized collection of records—and sit it on that the mysterious music-broadcasting box, her record player. She'd put on her favorites, including Louis Armstrong's "Blueberry Hill." The words didn't make sense to me, and I had no idea what that song meant, but its melody—along with the bowls of fruits, nuts, and hard old people candy that Sister put out throughout the home—kept our hearts full and merry.

Those were the days. Days full of family and fun times that I had grown accustomed to. Our tight-knit family loved one another, and this was how it was supposed to be—or so I thought.

CHAPTER 2

NEW HOME, NEW FAMILY

The summer of 1985 had just begun, and it was time to leave Woodcroft.

Having loaded her car full of suitcases, Ms. Jay headed for the door with me in tow. "Kee, you sure you got everything?"

"Yes, Mom," I responded, holding my favorite dollhouse game in one hand and her hand in the other.

Mother turned around and called out loudly, "Sister, we're about to go!"

Sister came out of her bedroom, dressed in a pink robe, and hurried toward us to see us off.

Ms. Jay hugged her. "Thank you. Thank you so much for everything, Sister," she said tearfully. "I don't know how I could have made it without you.".

"I pray that God blesses your journey, baby girl. It's going to be okay," Sister squeezed her arm. "As for your son, he'll be just fine here until you're ready for him." They hugged again with faces wet with tears. "You take good care of Lilbits, you here." She looked down at me and kissed my forehead.

We started down the steps, and I turned around to wave at Sister again.

"I love you, Lilbits!" she called out over the widening distance between us, and I smiled.

"Thanks again, Sister, for everything!" Ms. Jay responded in equal volume as she left Sister's place for good. She had finally landed her first apartment, and today was our move-in date. She was excited to finally be on her own, and I was excited for her.

As we drove off, windows down and the wind in our face, I began to wonder. Something wasn't quite right. "Mom, why can't my brother go with us to our new house?" I asked.

She hesitated a moment before answering me. "Because Sister is going to watch him while I go to work."

"Hm, but who's going to watch me? Why am I the only one going with you?"

"I'm going to watch you," she said. "I have arranged it so that you can go with me to cosmetology school, and your Auntie Janice will be coming over to watch you while I go to work."

"Well, why can't she watch my brother too?" I asked. "That's not fair! I want to go back and get my brother!" I began to get upset as I realized that we shouldn't have left him.

Ms. Jay pulled over the car and, looking back to the rear seat where I was, reassured me. "Don't worry, okay? He'll be coming over. It's just right now he's too young and he's going to be staying with Sister until he gets a little older."

I didn't quite understand what she meant at that moment, only that it was some kind of promise that my brother would join us some time in the future. To that promise I clung, and soon I was distracted by scenes of our new neighborhood.

Jackson Ward. It was just a mile from the Virginia State Capitol in Richmond.

I remember pulling into that place and thinking it looked somewhat like a jungle. Loud music blasted through the streets that were filled by more people than I could keep track of. People were everywhere. Young and old, girls and boys. The apartments all had a brick exterior and all looked the same—painted in a bright funny color and lined with litter and trash cans, some overturned, some filled to the brim. People didn't seem to mind, though. A fire hydrant was uncapped as the water shot out. Both children and grown-ups played in the water. Some grown-ups stood off in one group arguing, and others seemed relaxed in their conversation on the doorsteps. All unfazed by the hodgepodge of theater that captivated my full attention. I watched it all in stunned silence as we drove past them.

We came to a parking space, and Mom pulled over and parked her car. There was not much of luggage beside a big bag of clothing. "Just grab what you can," Mom said to me as she hauled the bag out of the trunk.

"Okay!" I said, taking a small tote that looked light from the backseat. Then I stood obediently by the side of the car and waited for Mom.

She got all the stuff and came to the sidewalk where I was. "1261 St. James Street," she read from a piece of paper, "is our new address." She repeated to me, "Kee, we're looking for the numbers 1-2-6-1," while signaling for me to help her find the apartment.

But I was too intrigued by our surroundings to help. It looked like a trashy jungle—but one that had pure fun. I couldn't wait to get in the midst of all the excitement. Never had I seen so many people in one place. As we walked past a small group of young girls on the sidewalk, one said hi to me and smiled. I waved back at her, returning a smile and a greeting, and continued following my mother.

"1261, we found it!" Mom said.

We walked in and climbed some stairs, finally reaching our unit. She put her key in the door lock and opened it. "Go ahead, Kee."

I walked into our new home and stopped in the middle of the living room floor. Putting down my bag in front of my feet, I looked around. I couldn't move. My eyes wandered from the floors and the walls, to the kitchen and the hallway. "This place surely is different from Sister's," I said to myself. Noticing the painted brick walls, I suddenly became cold and wanted to go back home with Sister. But Mother apparently felt differently.

"Come on, let's go and have a look at your new bedroom," Ms. Jay said, her eyes still shone brightly from the excitement of being on her own finally.

But I wasn't too thrilled about this bare, empty space. Even if I did have my own bedroom, that didn't matter to me. I was used to sharing a room full of people. I felt safe that way. At least I knew that ghosts could not kidnap me without getting beaten up by my cousins. I was cold and alone now, a feeling I just couldn't shake. And I certainly did not want to sleep in that bedroom by myself. I stood in the empty bedroom, expressionless and unable to even pretend to be happy. I so wanted to go back home.

I couldn't understand Mom's excitement. Surely, she must have loved our family as much as I did. Then why would she choose to move away, leaving everybody? Why doesn't she want to go back home?

Noticing my unenthusiastic reaction, she suggested, "Come on, let's go have pizza." Knowing how much I loved food, she knew that pizza would get my spirits up.

And it worked. My sad and lonely mood instantly turned into excitement. I shot my arms up in the air and agreed loudly. "Yes!" My spirits were immediately livelier, and I could now listen to Mom as she began talking about shopping for new furniture.

She grabbed her keys, and we headed for the door. As we walked back to the car, I noticed the same girls still standing on the sidewalk. We waved to one another again. Then the tallest one called out to me. Even though we had not met before then, she was already my friend. It was as though we had always known each other.

"Can I talk to her, Mom?" I asked.

"Sure," she said. "Don't be long. I'll wait in the car."

She knew I needed friends and didn't mind giving us a few minutes to become acquainted.

"You live around here?" asked my new friend.

"Um, yeah. Me and my mom just moved around here today."

"Well, my name is Patrice. What's your name?"

"Hi Patrice, my name is Keisha."

"Do you have sisters?"

"No, I don't. I just have a little brother, but he's not here yet."

Patrice introduced me to the girls with her. Two were her younger sisters, and the third girl was their friend. Patrice was seven and her sisters were five and six years old. Their friend was also seven. Before I had to run back to Mom, Patrice asked if I could come outside and play. I told her that Mom and I were going for pizza and I wasn't sure when we'd be back. Patrice invited me to come find her when we got back. Pointing to a house about 200 feet down the street, she said, "That's where I live." I told her I would if Mom let me. We then exchanged our goodbyes and I went back to the car to join Mom.

As I was buckling myself in, Mom said, smiling, "I see, you made new friends already. That's good."

"Yeah, that was Patrice. Mom, can I play with them outside when we get back from having pizza?"

"Sure, if it's not too late when we get back."

The day was figuring out pretty well. Pizza *and* new friends. The sorrow of being away from Sister and everyone else quickly faded in my mind. But before long Mom began to talk about the new apartment, which brought it all back.

"So what do you think of the new place?

I didn't know how to answer that question other than truthfully. "Ma, I really don't like it." Once I started, I had more to say than I thought I was capable of. "It's way too much trash everywhere and it's not like Sister's place. But there are a lot of people for me to play with. That's just about the only thing. I love our family, and now it seems like we're not going to be family any more since we've moved away from everybody."

Mom listened, looking surprised at my reaction. "It's only temporary, I promise. We will get a better one soon."

"Ma, it's ok for now," I said. "But I can't wait to see our new place. Just as long as it doesn't look like the one we just moved into."

She laughed. She found the humor in it, but I was as serious as I could be.

After we got home from our pizza dinner, it was still early enough for me to go out and play. Patrice was already outside. On my first day outside, I made five new friends, all of whom were introduced to me through Patrice. We played as if we had known one another for a long time. They showed me how to play Double Dutch, a game of jumping rope using two ropes. It was hard for me to catch on at first. I kept getting hit by the ropes while trying to jump in, and I thought of the genius idea of standing in between the ropes before they started swinging them and jumping like a monkey, with both of my legs going from side to side high in the air. Everybody laughed. They got used to me jumping that way after a while. It didn't matter to me though; it was all a part of the fun.

They also taught me how to play hopscotch, hide-and-seek, and "hide and go get it." The latter two games were alike, except hide-and-seek was all girls, and "hide and go get it" included boys. When we played "hide and go get it," we'd first pick the getter, who would cover and close his eyes while we ran. He would count to ten while we looked for our hiding spots. After counting to ten he could open his eyes and try finding us. That was the fun part. When the boys found us girls, they humped on us as if we were boyfriend and girlfriend doing things grown-up boyfriends and girlfriends do.

Our neighborhood had a center for children, the Calhoun Center. The people there gave us kids free lunches that included turkey sandwiches, chocolate milk, and a snack. We played different activities there that were directed by the Calhoun Center's staff. There was also a gym for those of us who were athletic. On Friday evenings, dances were held in that same gym for us youth. A live DJ played music while we danced under dim lighting. We danced in the center of the floor as loud music blasted through the speakers. I found that I fit right in at my new home in Jackson Ward. I learned their way of life quickly.

My first summer in Jackson Ward was awesome. There were so many things to do in our new hood, although many were things that children shouldn't be into. We children imitated what we saw happening around our homes, in the heart of that project, because it was the norm and anyone who did the opposite would be picked on for being strange. One of the things I learned was fighting with people, but I only fought with one girl. I made friends of everyone I met in Jackson Ward, but for reasons unknown to me, we fought every time we saw each other, in the neighborhood, during school recess, or anywhere else. She was my only foe in the whole Jackson Ward, but I wasn't scared or bothered by this. Everyone else had foes too.

Besides fighting with my one foe, everything else was pure entertainment for this six-year-old. I soaked it all up as if I were watching television, only it was a live version. There was always something going on. My friends and I sat at the bus stop and watched the happenings of our surroundings. From enraged adults having fist fights to grownup men chasing and shooting at other men with guns, we witnessed it all as children. That bus stop on St. James Street seemed to be where everything popped off. Though the violence was frequent, it never deterred me from going outside on adventures with my friends. For some reason, our parents seemed not to mind letting us children roam unsupervised outside. It had become a normal way of life for me, as it was for everyone else. Maybe that's why Jackson Ward was labeled a "project." It was where a bunch of poor struggling blacks congregated, where there was nothing but violence and death in the streets; we were the project.

Despite the reality of our new place, Mom and I bonded and enjoyed our newfound closeness away from everyone else. We spent so much time together doing all sorts of things. One of our favorite things besides pizza was movie night. Ms. Jay and I would agree on a new movie to rent that we'd never seen. We would then go to Blockbuster to look for and rent it.

One mid-summer day, we decided on *The Color Purple* for our movie night. It was one of the most talked-about movies at that time, and we both wanted to see it.

Movie night began with Mom popping fresh popcorn for us like they did at the movies. As she prepared the popcorn, one bowl for her and one for me, because I preferred buttery popcorn that she thought would not help her maintain her figure. I'd always laugh at her whenever she told me she needed to watch what she ate, because in my eyes she was as skinny as a pencil to me and really could afford to eat extra of everything.

While Mom busied herself in the kitchen, I made my own preparations: going to my room to retrieve my choice snuggle blanket. I situated myself comfortably on the couch with the blanket and waited for her—and the popcorn. She handed me my bowl and put hers down in her lap. Finally, when all was in order, Mom pushed the button on the remote, and the movie began.

We watched attentively. It was good at the start, but quickly it turned disturbing. I didn't understand it all, but I thought the old man was nasty for the way he treated and abused the young girl. "Where was her mother?" I thought to myself. I couldn't understand why any mother would allow her daughter to be with a grown man. Boy, was I glad to not have a mother like that. "I curse you!" Ms. Celie said to Mr. Albert on our little TV screen. "Until you do right by me, everything you think about is gonna crumble!" Before I found out how it would all end, we were interrupted by a knock on the door.

We looked at each other surprised, because we hadn't expected guests. Mom jumped up and paused the movie.

"Who is it?" she said, approaching the door.

"It's Pete," a muffled male voice answered from the other end.

Not quite hearing the stranger the first time, Mom asked again, "Who is it?" as she put her ear to the door because there were no peep holes.

"It's Pete, Jay," the man said again, only louder this time.

"Oh my God!" Mom covered her mouth in excitement. "Where did he come? How did he find me?" she asked herself a string of questions under her breath in quick succession. "Kee, how I look?" she asked me as she spun in a complete circle and nervously paced.

"You look the same, you know, how you looked before you got up," I said, trying to sound mature in giving my assessment.

"Don't be funny." She shot back with a smile as she stepped toward the door and opened it. Covering her mouth again, she squealed and jumped into the arms of the stranger, not once acknowledging the two little girls standing next to him. It was clear Ms. Jay and the man knew each other.

"When did you get back?" she asked, pulling back to have a good look of his face.

"I've been back a couple of months now," he said, and they started to hug again.

"Oh, my goodness! I've missed you!" Ms. Jay said, locked in between his arms.

Seeing that they were still focused on each other, I stood to my feet to play the host to the girls. I walked over to them, who had been standing expressionless by the man, and introduced myself. "Hi," I said to the tallest girl. "What's your name?"

"My name is Jasmine, and this, my sister, her name is Bella. That's Pete, our dad," she said, pointing at the man who was still occupied with Ms. Jay.

That was strange to me. They looked nothing like Pete. They looked like Korean dolls or something, I thought. "Oh, my name is Keisha and that's my mom." I gestured to the grown-ups busy catching up with each other. "How old are you?" I continued my questioning.

"I'm eight and she's five," she said. The younger girl wore her hair in these cute little pig tails. She had been standing quietly and chewing on the ear of her teddy bear.

"Does she talk?" I asked Jasmine.

"Yeah, she talks," she answered, elbowing Bella to coax her to say something.

Bella smiled at me and said a brief "hi," waving her hand timidly and still chewing on the ear of her bear.

Now Ms. Jay and Mr. Pete finally remembered us girls. Mom introduced me to Mr. Pete, and he introduced the girls to Mom. By now Mom and I had forgotten the good movie we were watching. Instead, we were as excited about the three visitors who now stood in our living room as they were eager for our attention.

The girls and I quickly became acquainted like the girl friends we had never been. Leaving Mom and Mr. Pete alone, I led the girls to my room for playtime. I showed them my toys and we carried on as kids would. Even though Bella and Jasmine looked different from me, we played as if we came from the same parents, and our fun lasted for hours. It had gotten late when Mom and Mr. Pete came into my bedroom.

Before they could say anything, I blurted out. "Mr. Pete, please don't tell me y'all about to go!" I pled, but politely. I was pleasant and smart. I was taught by my great-grandmother to be a child who minded her manners and respected adults.

He smiled as Mother answered me. "No, they're not about to go. We came to your room to tell you girls that you all are staying the night." She smiled at Jasmine and Bella.

"What about Mr. Pete? Is he staying the night too?" I asked my mother.

"Yes, he's staying too."

"Yay!" the girls and I shot up our arms in the air in unreserved glee—playtime was *not* over after all.

My mother walked over to my dresser and pulled out sleeping gowns for our little visitors. "These are for you girls to change into before bed."

After giving us the usual spiel about brushing our teeth and not playing too much longer, Mom and Mr. Pete kissed us good night and left us in my bedroom. We didn't hear from them the remainder of the night.

That was the first of many nights that soon turned into every night. As the girls' belongings piled up in our apartment, Mom started caring for them as if they were her own children. She cooked and we enjoyed family meals. She'd dress us all up and do our hair in bows. We went places together like a family.

Then the big announcement came. It had become official—Mom and Mr. Pete told us they were now officially a couple and we were all one big happy family living together. I was elated. We all were. Our home had now become theirs also. The girls and I hugged one another tightly while managing to jump up and down like the floor was a trampoline. The news meant endless playtimes for us. Plus, we were officially sisters now. And the man who used to be Mr. Pete had become Dad, and I was happy calling him that. That was what his own girls called him, and it made me feel closer to them all.

Every day my new sisters and I headed out for all sorts of fun, mischief, and adventure. I showed them things in the projects they hadn't known before. From sneakers dangling from the power lines to the street corners where different people every day huddled and argued and played, we found fun every direction we turned. The project swamped with what seemed like thousands of people, which was a constant source of new discoveries for us kids.

I introduced Jasmine and Bella to my friends, and it was love right from the beginning for all of us girls. Our circle of friends grew larger, and what they say is true—the more, the merrier. We showed my new sisters the cute boys who often hung around us. We taught my sisters how to play Double Dutch and how to cheer. On Friday evenings the girls and I got permission from our parents to join the cuties at the Calhoun Center for dances. We taught the girls Chinese knock-knock, one of our favorite games, using Huck Buck Marie's door. She was an old scary lady known for chasing children playing knock-knock away from her door.

She carried a broom and ran fast after the kids like a witch. She never talked, only chased the hardheaded kids who pestered her.

In the summer, somehow the fire hydrants were opened up almost daily. I learned after growing up that one could get arrested for opening up the fire hydrant for fun, but as a kid I joined children from all over Jackson Ward to have fun in the sun and the pressurized water sprouts from the hydrant. Loud music filled the air as we danced and chased each other, soaked wet from head to toe.

Even though the neighborhood was undeniably rough, we children created fun and were always entertained. We were never frightened of our environment, being already accustomed to the inevitable scenes that were, in our mind, simply one of many features of our neighborhood.

Days turned into nights and nights into days. Before I knew it, the last month of the summer had quickly breezed by, and it was time to go back to school. Almost everyone loved the beginning of a new school year, some more than others because of the fancy outfits their parents put together. Whatever each family's situation, the entire neighborhood prepared and things simmered down. Only the sound of crickets could be heard on the night before school.

Mom and Dad enrolled the girls in my school, adding to my excitement for a new school year. My two sisters had become my bus mates, although some of my friends took separate buses. School was fun enough, and I had great friends with me all throughout the day.

The arrows of time shot by more quickly than I could keep track. Thanksgiving arrived with a blink of an eye, then Christmas. No longer did I awaken to family that I knew and always surrounded me. Instead of Sister, my uncles, aunts, and cousins, my family now was Mom, Dad, and my sisters, and I didn't have a problem with that.

* * *

ON A CHILLY December morning, after a night of festive meal with family, I woke earlier than everyone else. Dressed in a long john two-piece night set with bells and bows all over, I awakened the girls so I wouldn't be alone going into the living room. There the tree stood, still beautifully decorated and tucked in the corner the way it had been the night before.

The smell of ham and chitterlings was still heavy in the air. Our eyes moved from one place to the next, hoping for and finding what was not there the previous evening: three giant stuffed stockings hung from the windowsill, each labeled with one of our names, and gifts spread out on the living room floor, extended from under the big, brightly lit tree.

We were all excited, but we had different goals—Bella ran toward the gifts while Jasmine and I headed for our stockings. Although we went to bed the previous evening with an inkling of the excitement to come in the morning, we had no idea this would be what we'd wake up to. All winter we hoped for a really great Christmas, and it was the best. There were so many different gifts. Gifts of all shapes and sizes. We had a ball ripping them all open. Clothes, and then toys. Shoes, and then more toys. Mom and Dad soon joined us in the living room and laughed as they watched us tear through the wrapping paper of our gifts. We spent what seemed like forever going from one gift to the next. It seemed as if Mom and Dad bought and wrapped an entire store.

We spent the remainder of that Christmas Day playing, eating, and more playing. Our room had become overfilled with more toys, clothes, and shoes. We all were happy. We had everything children could need and want. Our affectionate parents loved each other and provided all of life's necessities for us. Most importantly, we had one another, sisters for life. There wasn't much more we could ask for, other than a bigger room that would more comfortably accommodate us three girls and all of our things.

CHAPTER 3

TURN OF EVENTS

Life continued blissfully for the next couple of years, except we girls got older and taller. But slowly, through little changes, Mom and Dad started to become different people. At some point, they were no longer the loving couple who were always happy, always gazing into each other's eyes with love, who showered us with so much love and attention. They were still Mom and Dad, but they grew apart from each other and became distant from us girls. Before we could understand what was happening, life as we knew it came to a complete halt. Family dinners went from daily full-course meals to sugar and syrup sandwiches, if even that. Family shopping trips to the mall likewise were a thing of the past. Everything changed.

Initially, these changes didn't affect my sisters and me at all. The love we had for one another had overcome all of the drastic changes. We seemed to adjust quickly to the different dynamic at home, paying little heed to what was transpiring or where things were headed. The lack of food at home didn't bother us enough to even discuss it among ourselves.

But it wasn't because we noticed nothing. We observed it all. We began to notice these long, skinny, clear tubes with orange caps that were all over the place. On the floor, by the kitchen sink, on the sofa. We didn't know what they were, and we didn't mind them, really. When one was in the way we'd just toss it.

Mom no longer cooked. By this time, she and Dad were always in their room, with the door shut, quiet as mice. It only meant freedom for us to roam and do things children normally do. My sisters and I carried on, content in the love we had for one another. But even our little world of innocence and simple happiness would come crashing down.

Mom and Dad had a guy friend who had his own place. He didn't have a girlfriend like most boys did. He lived alone in a tall building not far from us that looked like a hotel but was really an apartment building, with many floors and countless apartments on each floor. There were no walls inside of his place. Only a big open room that had a tiny kitchen, a bed, a sofa, and a bathroom. We started going there quite frequently.

It began with regular visits from all of us, but before long, Mom and Dad began to simply drop us off. We didn't know or understand why. They just did. Most times we were forced to spend the night because they wouldn't come back for us.

One night, after playing with Jasmine and Bella at this man's place for some time, I was tired and could no longer fight the sleep that overcame me. My last sight before my heavy eyes shut close for the night was Dad's friend watching us with a can of beer in his hand. The three of us slept sweetly and deeply, our bodies closely nestled beside one another on the sofa. Dad's friend would sleep on his bed when we visited.

The more we came over, the more at home we felt. We even began going out into the hallways to play with the other children who lived in the building. We felt comfortable with Dad's friend and developed a natural trust in him. He treated us well and we had no reason to complain to our parents about going to his place.

But I still couldn't shake off the discomfort I felt when I saw him, with my sleepy eyes, watching us with a beer in hand. Soon, he offered to change places, letting my sisters and me sleep in his bed and he'd sleep on the sofa. We took him up on the offer immediately—there would be a lot more room for us three girls, and the bed was next to a huge floor-to-ceiling window he kept open at night to let in the breeze.

Everything about the first night he climbed into bed with us remains vivid in my memory. I was awakened from my sleep by his movement onto the bed, but I quickly realized what was happening. I lay stiff where I was, wondering why he got in bed with us, why the apartment was so dark, why everything was dead silent. I pretended to still be asleep, frozen as a mannequin. I was confused, but I knew boys weren't supposed to lie in bed with girls, not unless you're like Mom and Dad—two grown people who wanted to lie in bed with each other.

Night after night, he'd climb into bed with us and touched us in unfamiliar, creepy ways. In the darkness of the night, we lay still, scared and confused. But we dared not question him. We were taught to respect adults and respect them because they were our elders. I was never taught what to do in a situation like this. For all I figured, I still had to show that same respect. I didn't know if speaking up or asking any questions would get me in trouble—he might tell Mom and Dad I was disobedient or headstrong. So we remained quiet. Bella and I held each other's hands as a way to communicate to each other we were in this confusion together. Our silence sometimes gave way to weeping, but quietly we endured it all.

The man would talk to us casually the next morning and told us to keep "our little secret." Keeping it a secret we did, and I'd never forget the smell of beer strong on his breath when his dark shadow loomed over us. Even with the miserable experiences I would encounter later in life, nothing repulses me more than memories of those nights with this man.

One way Bella and I shielded ourselves from the repeated exploitation was by locking ourselves in the bathroom and sleeping there for the night. The cold bathroom floor beat the comfort of the soft bed, offering us refuge from our abuser. Jasmine, though, didn't seem to mind sleeping in the bed with him.

We never told anyone about what happened many nights in that apartment. In between visits to our "babysitter," we did our best to forget what that place meant to us. Soon, it didn't seem like that much of a big deal. We rolled with whatever life threw at us—parents growing apart, hungry stomachs, creepy babysitter—and adjusted to it all. But even as we did our best to rise to the challenges that required a strength beyond our years, things fell apart to such a degree that I no longer knew how to be happy.

A huge and loud argument between Mom and Dad erupted on a day close to my twelfth birthday, resulting in their split and the beginning of real horror for me. Before the split, I had my sisters to lean on and laugh with. The formerly happy family was now torn in two, and Dad moved away with my sisters. I was alone. Truly alone. Perhaps it helped that I still had Mom, but she had become different. She didn't seem to care as she did before about where I was, what I did, where I was going. How she dressed changed. Mom used to be a diva—a sweet, kind, beautiful diva, happy and full of life. She used to take pride in her appearance, which she took care to maintain. From her hair and nails to coordinated clothes and shoes. Not anymore.

Even her love of music and singing had faded.

I fell in love with the singer Prince at a young age because of Mom. He was her favorite, and she played his music every day. She would sing his songs with her velvety and expansive voice, and I would feel as if she was performing for me. She would grab something and sing into it as though it were a mic, just like she did at Sister's for family gatherings, and I was her audience. She also imitated Prince's movements and mannerisms, and I loved her performances. At some point before her split from Mr. Pete, she stopped singing and imitating Prince.

All that changed. Mom was a different Mom now. Angry, irritable, and soon she'd become worse, and I would be the only one home to diffuse her bitter, violent outbursts.

One beautiful warm day, around the middle of the day I was out playing with my friends. Being the children that we were, we stuck to the cheers and games we were familiar with, and Chinese knock-knock was the game of choice. I was chosen to knock on somebody's door, after which we'd all run. Never did it dawn on me it was a poor choice to play this game in the vicinity of the apartment Mom and I shared.

Apparently, the lady whose door I knocked on had enough of being a victim of Chinese knock-knock and didn't hesitate to let my mom know after she saw me running away. When I got home not much later, I sensed right away the tension in the apartment. Mom looked at me with mad eyes, her fury heated enough to set herself on fire. I was scared—never had I seen her this angry before.

She stopped me in my tracks on my way to get a drink of water. "What were you doing outside?"

I paused. I knew the lady must have told on me, and I felt stupid that a game of Chinese knock-knock would get me in trouble. Although I could sense the heat of Mom's anger, I gave her the truth. "Me and my friends were outside playing a game."

"A game," she repeated, even more irate, as though she were about to explode. "How the hell is knocking on somebody's door and running a game? Answer me!" she screamed.

I wanted to crawl under a rock and hide. I was scared for my life and started trying to explain. But she turned her back on me and went into the kitchen. In a few seconds she returned, with a chair in her hand. She sat the chair down in front of her and took out a black cord. I had no idea what was about to take place. All I knew was that I was in fear. I continued trying to explain but she interrupted me.

"Lay your ass down on this chair, because you are about to pay for your disrespect."

Disrespect. I had no idea how I disrespected anyone. I was taught to always mind my manners. In fact, I continued to be respectful to Mom even in that moment of confusion and fear, and I did exactly as she instructed. I lay down on my stomach across the chair.

"You're going to learn your lesson today," she said as she hit me with her first strike.

The cord landed on the back of my thigh, right under my butt. It stung with a burning feeling that I couldn't describe. It was the worst pain imaginable. I had been whipped with a belt before, but it was no comparison with a television cord. Every lash on my skin was more painful than the one before. Mom beat me as if she was taking something out on me, and I couldn't understand. I thought I was her baby, I thought she loved me. Love didn't hurt someone like this. Love shouldn't feel like hate. I screamed in agony as the pain from the electrical cord pierced my entire back side. All the more hurtful, it was my *mother* who was beating me this way, relentlessly, furiously, ruthlessly, as if I were her worst enemy.

I finally got up because I could no longer bear the pain. I ran to the nearest corner and balled up to protect my face in case she continued beating me.

"Did I tell you to get up?" she said as she continued her striking.

The cord landed on my head, my legs, my back, the side of my face that my arms couldn't cover. Anywhere and everywhere she could hit me I was hit. Then she stopped, finally.

Scared and confused as I had never been before, I dared not move.

I stayed in the corner, balled up with my head buried in my lap, until I heard her walk away. As I stood up, adding to the sensations of fear and confusion, I was in disbelief when I looked down at my arms and legs. Blood oozed from the fresh ripped-open wounds that covered my body. The pain I felt from the bottom of my stomach was worse than the pain from the wounds. Tears streamed down my face as my body shook. Why? Why did she do that? The one person that I thought loved me. That one person that I thought had my back. That one person who gave birth to me, nursed me, taught me to speak, made me popcorn. That person. That very same person also just hurt me in a way I never would've envisioned. That person, Ms. Jay, my mother.

She returned, but I was too exhausted to even feel afraid. "Now go in the bathroom and clean yourself up," she said, still irritated, but not at all remorseful. It didn't bother her to see my flesh ripped and bleeding.

I made my way to the bathroom, taking each step in pain, and I was too scared to look up at her when I walked past her. That day, the innocent, unwavering trust I had always had in her died. Even when my sisters and I frolicked on empty stomachs and slept in the home of an abusive babysitter that Mom had handed us to, I trusted her. Mom loved me, and I never questioned that. No longer, though. That was the day when I stopped resting in the assurance of her love for me, and that was the day that started Mom's tireless ill treatment of me.

In the bathroom, I looked at myself in the mirror and broke out in sobs again. In between my sniffles, I saw more and more wounds on my body that I hadn't noticed in the living room. I was hurting inside and out, but my sisters weren't there to comfort me. Nor was Sister, or any aunt, uncle, cousin, friend. Or my mother.

CHAPTER 4

RICHMOND'S SOUTHSIDE

I was twelve when Mom and I relocated to the south side of town. A change of scenery didn't mean that things between us had improved at all. Mom had not returned to her old self, and I still hadn't wrapped my head around how she became a different person. One good thing, though, was that I met a lot of new people in our new neighborhood, which provided some much-needed distraction. They were pretty cool. All of them. But one chick stood out more than others. Her name was Sonja.

Sonja and I met at Elkhardt Middle School. She was younger than I by one year, but she seemed older because she knew things I didn't. We became close quickly, sharing with each other the things that we went through at home. I listened when she told her stories, but I didn't know what to say in response most of the time. She would respond to my stories with comments like "That's crazy." I felt she understood me and was on my side.

Sonja lived in an apartment complex right next to ours. There was a wooden gate that separated the two complexes, but the gate was often kicked down, which made our visits to each other a lot easier. Where she lived was called Jefferson Village, but everyone I knew called it JV.

JV was a hood, not much different at all from Jackson Ward, except the buildings didn't have a brick exterior. I felt like I fit right in because of the similarities it had with my old hood.

Every day after school, Sonja came to fetch me from my house and we spent time at her place, where there were a lot more to do. We talked a lot, but our conversations were hardly what one would expect to hear from typical children. We both had troubles at home and felt comfortable confiding in each other. I tried to the best of my ability to explain to Sonja how my mother changed. How things had gone from great to terribly bad. How Mom wasn't buying me clothing or shoes I needed for school, or for anything. How there was never food in the house. I told her our electricity was always being shut off and I couldn't understand why.

One day, after listening to me describe the situation at home in detail for the first time, Sonja politely said, "Oh girl, your mom is on drugs, and it sounds like she smokes crack."

"Crack, what is that"? I hadn't heard of that drug, or any drug for that matter.

"Oh, crack is a drug old people use to get high. They get hooked on it and spend all their money on it. I know because my mom smokes crack and she's been doing it for a while. And just like you, me and my sister barely get anything new. She never sells her food stamps though. And our lights never get cut off," Sonja said casually. "But everything else you said sounds just like my mom." The nonchalance in her voice was as shocking as what she just told me.

Dumbfounded, I couldn't respond. I took a few minutes to process the information. "So that's what's wrong with my mom," I thought to myself. She was on drugs. "Where do these drugs come from?" I asked Sonja. "Like how do they get the drugs?"

"I don't know. All I know is that the dudes you see standing outside all the time sell drugs. Young dudes and old ones too."

It all was beginning to make sense to me. I never knew why some people always hung around out on the streets in Jackson Ward and JV. I knew now they were selling drugs or even doing them. Everything Sonja said matched my mom's behavior, but I struggled to put two and two together. Unlike Sonja's mom, my mom worked. I didn't care how she got into drugs, but it was hard to believe she would get paid and spend all her money on drugs. In order to get crack or whatever she was using, she neglected me and my needs. She didn't get me any new school supplies or replace my worn-out shoes that I had long ago outgrown. By the time we moved to BlueRidge, holidays had become the saddest time of the year. I didn't even bother expecting any gifts. It would be a great Christmas if Mom fed me or didn't take out the television cord.

I decided to test Sonja's theory that Mom was using drugs and spending all her money on it. So, my investigations began. While mom was away at work, I started going through her dresser drawers looking for her check stubs. I couldn't find them at first, but I didn't give up. I wanted to see how much she made, which might explain our lack of money. Maybe—just maybe—she didn't make enough to cover the bills. I wanted to give Mom the benefit of the doubt, especially since we no longer lived in the projects and our new home might have more expensive bills.

If I didn't know anything else, I knew she got paid weekly. I searched till I finally stumbled across a few of her pay stubs in her drawer. The stubs read a few different figures, but all were more than I expected: $572, $703, $497, etc. I was only twelve, but I knew this would more than pay for bills and food. Just *what* had she been doing with all this money?

I was hurt, and angry. Sonja was right about Mom. The truth was in front of me, but I couldn't believe she was selfish enough to disregard my needs and spend it all on crack.

The next day, still in shock, I confided in Sonja about what I discovered. I also started paying attention to other things because I so badly wanted to understand what was happening and to regain Mom's attention. More proof than I wanted to see came my way. Perhaps it was always there if I looked for it.

One Friday evening I went home after being over at Sonja's. It was close to the time that my mom was expected to be there. I called out to Mom as I shut the door behind me.

"I'm in my room," she responded.

I quickly climbed the stairs and knocked on her closed door, eager to talk to her. There was this teenage club, Nite World, around the Southside that was extremely popular among the youth. On the weekends when it opened, everybody that was somebody was there, and all the girls would get dolled up for the guys to go party there. Sonja and I would go when we could come up with the money to cover us both. I was hoping this Friday we could go. "Mom, can I talk to you really quickly?" I tapped on her door.

"Hold on for a minute, Kee."

"Can I have some money to go to Nite World with Sonja?" I pressed my ear to the door and asked very politely.

"Yeah, just a second."

I sat on the step and anxiously waited. Five minutes turned into twenty, and twenty into thirty. I grew impatient. The club let out at 11:00 p.m. and it was already past 7:00. I didn't bother knocking this time, because she would just have me wait some more. I turned the door knob and stepped inside Mom's room.

It was all there, in front of me. The proof I wanted not to exist.

I stood watching it all with my mouth gaped open, in utter disbelief. To speculate that Mom smoked crack was one thing. But to see her smoking it was something different. She didn't even stop or try to hide it when she saw me. She had a crack pipe to her mouth with a lighter and fire at the opposite end of it. The smoke floated from one end of the pipe to the other, and she inhaled all of it. I lost my breath, unsure how to react, but my tears came rolling down without prompting.

She got up clumsily and grabbed twenty dollars from her night stand. She staggered a bit as she walked toward me. After putting the money in my hand, she shoved me out of her room and locked the door, all without a word to me.

I stood alone outside the room, unsure what I had just seen. But I smiled when I looked down in my hand and saw the money. I remembered what that meant—Nite World fun for Sonja and me. I wiped away the tears and rushed out the door to meet Sonja, forgetting—or trying to forget—what I had witnessed.

At the club, rhythmic music pumped up the atmosphere, energizing everyone and helping us all leave behind what troubles we'd brought to the club's doors. It was packed as always. The club room was dark and everyone was dancing. Sonja and I swayed to the music, grinding with the boys like I did back at the Calhoun dances. We showed our best moves.

This evening Sonja and I had another girl with us, her cousin Charlene. We all got our flirt on and danced the night away with one another and with boys. We had a ball that night, the way we did every time we could afford to go. But for Sonja and me, it was more than just regular fun for teenagers. The music, dance, and time with friends was also an escape from our problems back home. When the night ended, we were forced back to reality.

And reality turned worse over time. Mom went from somehow managing to keep a job to being on welfare and receiving food stamps. Still, there was never any food. I never asked questions because I was afraid to. Sonja knew about our situation and every day she would come get me to have dinner at her spot. Even though her mom smoked crack, she kept a fridge full of food and cooked every day.

At some point, Mom began going to a church and brought me along. Apparently, the trouble she was in couldn't be fixed on its own and she needed help. She sought the help of a pastor, thinking he would deliver her from her crack demons and help her return to the way she used to be back before Mr. Pete came along.

I was young, but I remember vividly how the pastor helped. Almost every time we went to church he'd pick Mom out of a crowd. "Jay, come up here," he called out to her in front of the entire church during Sunday morning services. "What is it you want the Lord to do for you?"

She whispered some words in his ear, after which he grabbed some oil and marked a cross with it on her forehead. Then, with her eyes shut and hands in the air, they both bowed their heads.

"Dear Lord. I thank you for my sister Jay, oh God. We come to you today asking a mighty thing of you. You said that if we believe on the name of Jesus, we could be set free of anything. I stand in agreement with my sister today, asking that you set her free." He then started calling out the names of Mom's demons one by one.

"Leave me alone!" a loud male voice came out of Ms. Jay. Her veins enlarged and bulged through her skin. With the strength she got out of nowhere, it took all of six men to keep her from strangling the poor pastor.

I sat on the front pew next to my aunt Janice, who had stayed close to Mom and me, witnessing something out of the *Exorcist* movie. Only it wasn't a movie—it was reality, and it was happening to my mom. I covered my eyes and turned away. I was scared for my life. Mom had monsters inside her, and I was scared to be alone with her.

All the theatrics didn't fix her problem. Her condition only seemed worse each time after the pastor's routine, as if the monster had left only to get friends to come join in on the party. The monsters had mom enraged for no reason, and, again, I was on the receiving end of her raging abuse.

Early one school morning I had gotten dressed and was about to head to the bus stop when she came into my room. She was angry, and she demanded that I wash the dishes and not go to the bus. I thought she was being nasty, and I couldn't understand what would have upset her so early in the morning. I looked at the clock and glanced out the window at the kids standing at the bus stop. "There's no way I'm going to wash those dishes and make it," I thought to myself. But I didn't have a choice. I hurried into the kitchen to begin the dishes.

In just a few minutes, Mom came into the kitchen, livid. I was nervous, unsure what I had done but certain of what was to come.

"You're hardheaded. I told you not to miss that damned bus. I'm going to fix you." But she turned around and walked away after those menacing words. "Hurry up with those dishes," she screamed as she headed for the living room, "and come in here when you are done."

Quickly, I finished up the dishes and immediately went over to the living room. There she stood in front of the very chair I was often beat in. In her hand was the same black cord she used to beat me. My mind instantly flashed to the many times before when I was made to take off my clothes and lay across that very chair. She would beat me until she drew blood and didn't mind doing it. This morning, though, I wasn't having it.

I grabbed my jacket and dashed for the door. I ran as fast I could from the house, as she screamed for me to come back from the doorway. I thought of how much I hated her, and how I was never coming back there if I could help it. I walked the entire way to school. When I got there, I told my longtime friend Akeelah why I was late.

It wasn't a total surprise for her. I often confided in her about the problems at home, and we'd been going to the same schools since elementary school. "That's it, girl," she said, incredulous. "You're going home with me. That lady is crazy!"

Akeelah was spoiled. She was an only child, and her mother made sure she stayed dipped in the latest fashions.

After school that day, I went back to her home with her. We ate snacks, talked about problems and nothings, and watched television. Their apartment was nicely furnished. It felt warm and inviting, a complete opposite of my mom's place. Ms. Jay's place was cold and bare. We were so poor that a trampoline replaced the glass top of our kitchen table where we ate. Besides being poverty-stricken, there was an evil presence in that place. I always felt someone watching me when I knew no one was there. I wanted so badly to leave and get away from that mean, evil lady who treated me as if I meant nothing to her. I would've jumped at the first chance of somebody taking me away.

Just when we began to notice our hunger, Akeelah's mother arrived. She brought dinner that she picked up from a restaurant. They invited me to stay for dinner, and I was only too happy to oblige. As we impatiently dug into the pizza, the focus of the chatter soon turned to my situation. I wasn't aware until that point that her mom knew all about me and what I was going through at home. She told me she was willing to take me from my mom if the abuse happened again. Boy, was that music to my ears, and I wanted so badly for that to happen right away. But she said she was going to take me back home that evening, and if it happened again she wanted me to call her. After dinner, Akeelah's mom gave me her phone number before taking me home.

When we pulled into a parking space in front of our home, my palms became sweaty and my heart pounded. There was no telling what Ms. Jay would do to me. For all I knew, she was prepared to beat me to pieces. But she just opened the front door to let me in and walked upstairs back into her room. The night ended in unexpected peace for me, but the relief was only temporary.

I didn't get the opportunity to move away. Over the next year or so, nothing changed, except weed was the new popular thing and mom had met a new lady friend. Her days of being in the house angry were over. I barely saw her around, but I didn't mind at all. Her absence meant freedom and no more abuse. But the new situation wasn't exactly ideal. Newly fourteen, I was scared to be in that old spooky place alone. Mom had the only key. If I ever left home for school or to meet friends outside, the door had to remain unlocked. I came and went, to school, to the store, to a friend's home, and rarely was Mom home when I got home. I was lonely, for sure, but I didn't feel it. Whatever was watching me was there too.

I saw Mom *maybe* once a week, twice if she wanted to change her clothing. Whenever she decided to make it home, she didn't come alone. She brought a party with her. But I had learned to separate my life from hers, and I turned a blind eye to what Mom was doing, at our home or elsewhere.

The new and complete focus in my life now was boys and smoking weed. Though I had never smoked before, I was willing to try because everyone was doing it. And although my virginity was intact—perhaps because of it—boys were still my interest. At any rate, any kind of attention was better than none. I dibbled and dabbed with boys a bit, but never anything serious. Just a little dry humping and grinding here and there, always with pants on.

One day, after school, Sonja showed up at my door. She told me her new boo was coming over that evening, and I was invited to smoke with them because he kept weed.

On our way to her crib, we both became excited about today being "the day"—our introduction to smoking. We entered Sonja's home through a back door and made our first stop in the kitchen, where we stopped to fix ourselves some dinner plates. I was always starving after school. The food they gave us there wasn't enough, and the fact that I only ate once after school didn't help either. While we ate in the living room, the knock on the door came. Sonja walked up to the door and looked through the peep hole. Then she turned and looked at me with the biggest grin on her face—it was her boo. She opened the door and welcomed him in.

I was surprised to see my cousin walk in. "Oh my God! Craig!" I hugged him in disbelief.

We hadn't seen each other in a while. He didn't seem to have changed much, but I noticed that behind his right ear was a big blunt already rolled. We spoke over each other as we were eager to get caught up on how our lives had been since we last saw each other. After Sonja and I finished up dinner, we all went outside on the front porch to smoke. Craig lit the blunt. He puffed it a few times and passed it to Sonja.

I just watched. I needed to know what to do. Never before had I attempted to smoke anything, or was I in the company of anyone else smoking. We were virgin smokers, Sonja and I—or so I thought. The way she pulled that blunt told me this wasn't her first time. She must've tried smoking with Craig already, I thought. After she pulled it twice, it made her cough, and she passed it to me. I was kind of nervous but I didn't show it. They both watched me like hawks, intently observing how I'd do with it. I gave them a feigned menace to act tough, like I wasn't as green as I was.

I hit the blunt and inhaled. It was easy. I showed them what I was made of; I was no punk smoker. I hit it twice more and started coughing as the smoke filled my fresh lungs. I passed it to Craig, not wanting to overdo it. The blunt was passed around once more before Sonja and I told Craig we had enough. He kept smoking. It took more for him to feel the effect because he was a pro. After half of it was gone, he put the blunt out, and we got back inside the house.

I don't think I realized the effects of weed. I didn't know what to expect. I wanted to ask Craig how the high was supposed to feel, because I was unsure if I was there. I decided against it because I thought he would laugh at how silly of a question it was.

Sonja popped a movie in the VCR. But for some reason everything seemed to be moving in slow motion. I started feeling strange. "Why is no one talking?" "The movie is so boring." Thoughts flashed through my head, and my heart started beating really fast. I grabbed my chest and panicked. I thought I was about to die. "Oh my God, what's happening to me?"

Craig looked at me with a silly grin on his face. I guess he had expected to see this typical first-timer reaction. "What's wrong, you alright?" he asked casually.

Scared to death, I shook my head no.

"Do you want to go outside and catch some air real quick?"

I nodded but was scared to talk. I stood up, and he rose with me, grabbing my hand to steady me. "Oh my God, I'm about to die. I can't breathe. What did you give me? What was in that weed?" I rambled through my quivering lips without pausing for him to answer. I was scared because my heart beat loudly and I could hear it. My ears rang, sounding like they were about to pop. The noise was in my head. At any moment I felt like I could drop dead. I didn't know what to do.

Craig smiled and said, "Come here, girl." He wrapped his arms around me. "Girl, you crazy," he said. "You're not about to die. Just chill and calm down. It's your first time smoking and you're high. That's all."

How could he be so calm, and why was he still smiling? There wasn't anything funny. My life was on the line. At any moment I could drop dead. This was serious. But if, and only if I lived, I was never going to smoke weed again. How could someone smoke something that made them feel like they were about to go away from here. But I did survive that day.

After I calmed down, Sonja and Craig walked me home, and I prepared myself for school the next day. Life went on, and weed didn't seem so scary anymore.

CHAPTER 5

NEW BEGINNINGS: HUSTLING AND MOTHERHOOD

A FEW MONTHS WENT BY SINCE I TRIED SMOKING FOR THE first time with Craig and Sonja. Still an adventurous eighth-grader, I was ready for new experiences. One day I was standing on my porch after school when I noticed a new group of boys in our neighborhood. One particularly cute guy stood out to me. I wondered where they were from and whose crib they were over. After noticing that same group a couple of times I figured out they were with Justin, one of my school mates. I knew him well, and soon I found an opportunity to get Justin alone.

"Hey Justin." I walked up to him in the hallway at school.

"What's up, Keisha?"

"Nothing." I got straight to the point. "Who were those dudes I saw you with yesterday at home"?

"Round Blue Ridge?"

I nodded.

"Oh, that's Jay and T and them. My cousins."

"Your cousins?"

"Yeah, those are my people. Why?"

"Well, what about the dark-skinned one with the low cut and waves. Who is that?"

"You talking about Jay. What about him?"

"I want to meet him. Hook me up, aight?"

With boys this age you could never know if they took you seriously, but only two days later Justin came to my house with Jay. I was surprised because he hadn't said anything to me about it. He just showed up with

Jay at my door step. Thank God my mom wasn't home. She wouldn't have approved of two teenage boys coming to see me.

I was extremely nervous being close to Jay. He was so fine, dressed nicely like a grown-up. Every time I saw him he was fly. Justin introduced us just as I asked. Boy, did I blush. I couldn't contain what I felt. Justin shook his head and walked off when Jay started talking to me.

"Hey, what's up?" Jay broke the silence.

I mumbled something in response. I was shy and at a loss for words. I thought I'd let him lead the conversation.

"How long you have been living around here?" he asked.

"About two years."

"Really, why have I never saw you before?"

"I don't know." Then I thought about it. It must have been because I was at Sonja's every day.

"How old are you?"

"I'm fourteen," I said. "What about you, how old are you?"

"Fifteen. You got a boyfriend?"

"No, I don't have a boyfriend. Do you have a girlfriend?"

"Naw, I don't have a girl."

The back-and-forth continued for a long time as we got to know each other, and the initial awkwardness disappeared. My hunger pangs had come and gone. We got on nicely, and we exchanged numbers before saying our goodbyes.

The more Jay and I talked, the more I like him. That cute bad boy image had me going. He started coming around my way more and more frequently, and the attention he was showing me told me that he liked me as well.

Out of the blue, one evening Mom showed up at home. She had been gone on one of her missions for quite a few days, out and about doing only God knows whatever, for money to buy cocaine with, and I hadn't seen her at all. This day, I was outside on the curb talking to Jay when she walked up. She embarrassed me with her presence because she didn't look like a functional mother.

"Hey ma," I acknowledged her despite my discomfort.

"Hey." Her reply was brief and pointy as she walked past us. I knew she disapproved.

After I was done talking to Jay, I went in the house. Mom was in the shower. I went in my room and lay across the bed with my door wide open, waiting to hear what she had to say about me talking to some boy. Did she expect that I, a young girl without a mom or dad, would sit alone at home?

She put on a night gown and came back to my door. "Who was that boy you were talking to?"

"That's just my friend Jay."

"Well, Jay needs to stay away from here. I don't like him." Without explaining herself, she walked away.

I thought to myself, "She doesn't like him. Right, she doesn't even know him. This lady is crazy. I don't ever see her. She doesn't feed me, doesn't buy me anything, pays me no attention. Now somebody else is paying me attention and she doesn't like it." I decided I would pay her no mind, as she paid me none. What she said went in one ear and straight out the other. When I got home from school the next day she was gone again.

Weeks and months passed when Jay finally popped the question, asking me to officially be his girl. Excitedly, I accepted, and we celebrated all day the day we became a couple. And with Mom gone again, I had more alone time with Jay. He came over almost every day now and we'd spend hours on the front porch, talking about our days, watching people in the neighborhood, and commenting on this person and that car. We fell harder for each other as we spent all this time together. Finally, one day Jay asked if he could come in my house.

I dreaded that question although I had expected it'd come. I was never thrilled about the idea of letting anyone in besides Sonja, because she knew my mom was on drugs. She knew my situation. Our place looked crazy poor, which I warned Jay. He didn't care.

It was true. He didn't care about the material things I lacked. He thought enough of me to make me his girl and he liked me regardless of what he saw, or did not see, inside our home. I led Jay upstairs to my bedroom since the ugly old small sofa was hideous and dirty-looking. In my room, we both sat on the bed. It felt only natural when Jay leaned over and kissed me. Not knowing how to kiss back, I did the best I could. He seemed to have enjoyed it, so we kept going. He unbuttoned my pants and pulled them down, but I got scared.

"Wait!" I stopped him.

"What, what's wrong?"

I was embarrassed. "I'm a virgin. I've never done it before."

"Okay," he said, "I'll take my time."

That reassurance didn't help me, but my young love for him overcame my fear and I allowed him to proceed. I lay still, not knowing what else to do.

Jay kept his word and was gentle, if persistent, as he tried again and again until he was inside of me. I bled, and I knew then I was no longer a virgin. That made me feel like a big girl. It took our relationship to another level.

I was excited and willing to please Jay whenever he wanted. To me it meant our relationship would only get better and last longer.

Mom was home one day when Jay popped up. When Jay knocked, Mom answered before I even knew he was there. I was in my room when she came upstairs and told me he was outside. She went back to her room quickly and shut the door behind her. I thought it was strange she didn't tell me to get Jay to leave because she didn't like seeing him around.

When I got outside he was smiling. That automatically put a huge smile on my face.

"Hey boo," he said, and I lunged into his arms.

We hugged and kissed. Jay knew that Mom didn't care for him. He and I had gotten rather close and I told him about it. But I told him she didn't seem to mind today that he came over to see me, which I thought was unusual.

Jay explained to me. "Your mom is a junkie and I gave her some coke to let me see you."

I was ashamed, humiliated beyond belief. I didn't know what to say but he read my expression.

"It's okay, boo. Sometimes things happen we can't control." He hugged me again.

After that day, Jay moved in—he earned that by feeding Mom coke. And Mom went from being gone several days at a time to always being home, she and her junkie friends. They all bought their drugs from Jay. Soon, I joined him. I had become his partner in crime. He taught me how to cut up and bag cocaine. He taught me the difference between a dime, a twenty, and a fifty of crack. He had given me the streets, and I took a liking to my new trade. I learned a lot about drugs and we made tons of money day and night. Our entire neighborhood and some of Sonja's bought drugs from us. Jay spoiled me with the cash we brought in. He bought me everything I needed and wanted. Clothes, shoes, money, new gold teeth. We were both living the life.

Most days, Jay was home with me, dealing drugs to what seemed like a never-ending stream of visitors at our doorsteps for a few grams. On a few days, though, I was alone. One of those times when Jay wasn't around, I heard Mom coming through the door. I was used to her coming and going, alone or with her party of friends. I didn't bother getting up to greet her. I stayed in my room cutting and bagging coke when Ms. Jay come up the stairs. She was loud. Though I heard other people's footsteps, I only heard her voice. When I thought all her people were in her room with her, I got up to go to the bathroom, which was next door to my bedroom.

When I opened my bedroom door, I saw two guys I had gone to school with standing in the hallway. My mom's bedroom door was shut. Apparently, she was in the room with a third person. The look on their face made it all clear to me—they were waiting their turns; my mother was selling herself in exchange for drug money.

This was the embarrassment of my life, seeing my mom with people my age engaging in these shameful activities. Mortified, I shut my door and sat on the edge of my bed. I didn't even understand why my feelings were hurt. But they were, and I cried. I couldn't leave my bedroom until they were gone. That day, I lost all respect for Ms. Jay. She might have given birth to me, but she was nothing more than a stone-cold crack whore junkie who'd do anything for a high.

Jay had a different experience with his parents. He came from a two-parent family and his mother had a good job at a well-established cigarette plant, where she worked some 12-hour but mostly 16-hour shifts. She was never home, and when she was, she slept. Jay's dad let him and his twin brother do what they wanted. They were spoiled. They didn't have to be in the streets but they wanted to, so they did. They had tons of friends and were very popular. They were the young life of Fulton Hill, where they were from.

When Jay and his twin brother turned 16, they each got a brand new car as birthday gifts. Jay's vehicle was a little blue jeep. His brother's was a red car. Jay and I both loved his car. Jay wasted no time teaching me how to drive. And before I knew it, I was driving that thing all over the place as if I had been driving for years. We thought we were grown-ups. We had a new car and a steady income, and we could afford to do whatever we wanted. We felt unstoppable.

One evening I was preparing myself for school. Mom was home getting her rest before she hit the streets again for her missions. She sat on the edge of her bed with her door wide open. I was fixing my hair, standing naked in front of a full-length mirror, and she watched me.

"Come here," she said.

I stopped what I was doing to my hair and walked over to her.

She, touching the bottom of my stomach said, "You're pregnant, and I want you to make an appointment to go to the doctor."

I was stunned. "There's no way I'm pregnant," I thought. "I'm only fifteen, and there's no way I'm carrying a baby."

The next day Mom gave me the number to my doctor and my insurance card. I called and set an appointment for the following week. Jay came with me because I told him what mom said.

At the doctor's office they ran all kinds of tests, the ones they give sexually active females. "Negative, negative, negative, positive" were the results the doctor read to Jay and me.

"Positive, what do you mean positive? What's positive?" I asked the doctor.

"Everything was negative, the chlamydia, gonorrhea, and syphilis. Only your pregnancy test was positive. You're ten weeks pregnant, young lady. Now when you leave this room, I need you to set an appointment at the front desk to come back and see me for regular prenatal care during the course of your pregnancy. Here are some materials for you to read to familiarize yourself with what to expect. Every new mom needs these." With that, the doctor left the room.

Jay and I were stunned but happy. We looked at each other in amazement before we came to and hugged and kissed each other. I was only fifteen when I became pregnant for the first time. I didn't think about what it would mean to have a baby. I didn't consider how I'd finish school or how I would even care for this child. All I knew was that I was carrying Jay's baby, and I was happy.

When I got to the crib Mom wasn't there. I rushed to Sonja's house and gave her the news. Rubbing my belly, I told her what happened at the doctor's office, the tests and the "diagnosis," but I still couldn't believe there was life inside of me. When Jay and I had sex, never once did it cross my mind that I could get pregnant. My young mind didn't think to consider the consequences of sex. Neither had I had anyone to break down what happened when the birds and the bees got together. What Jay and I were doing just felt right, and in that moment, nothing else mattered.

In the next couple of days, Mom was out of sight, out of mind. Jay and I continued selling drugs and running the home, as if we were grown and had things under control. Jay and I started going back and forth between my Aunt Janice's house down the road and Mom's house. Aunt Janice also smoked crack, as did Mom, but she was always there for me and was a steadfast friend to me. We made good money at both places, and I confided many things in Aunt Janice, including news of my pregnancy.

One day when Jay and I were over at my aunt's place, Mom came for a visit. This was the first time I saw her after going to the doctor's. I was nervous to tell her. After failing to figure out the best way to break the news to her, I decided to be straightforward. I went over to the kitchen, where she was drinking a glass of water.

"Ma, I'm pregnant."

She nearly choked on her water. She stopped and turned around to look at me. "You what?" she said as if she hadn't heard me correctly, as though she wasn't the one to first notice my belly or the one to tell me I needed to see a doctor.

"I'm pregnant," I repeated.

Instantly she got angry and squinted her eyes. I saw the look of rage that was always in her eyes whenever she was ready to beat the hell out me.

"Don't think you're going to keep it. You're going to get rid of it as soon as possible," she said to me.

I wanted so badly to say to her that she couldn't tell me what to do, because she was nothing more than a junkie, and that if I had to, I'd go live somewhere else before I got rid of my baby.

Over the next couple of days, Aunt Janice, my mom, and mom's old flame Pete (my former "stepdad") had heated discussions about my pregnancy. I didn't even know where Pete had come from, but I didn't care. No one could change my mind. After some struggle and many protracted family meetings, Mom decided to allow me to go through with the pregnancy.

They got together and started making plans for my baby shower. I didn't know how that was going to work because they all smoked crack and couldn't hold on to any money. My estimated due date was October 31. That time rolled around quickly and I gained a lot of weight. I gave birth on October 25, 1993, five days after I turned 16. Jay was right by my side the entire time. He named our son CeQuan. He was a funny-looking little fella. He was long and thin, weighing only six pounds and seven ounces.

Three days after CeQuan's birth, we were released from the hospital. Back at home I found the environment no longer appealing to me. It felt dirty and unfit for a newborn. But I stuck with it because the money continued flowing in. Ms. Jay continued with her smoking cocaine in the same house with my new son. Our customers showered us with love after we returned from a few days away at the hospital, and our income doubled in less than a week. Some of our customers paid us in jewelry, and I began a collection of diamond rings and other precious stones. With all our money, my baby had everything that a mother could want for her child. Plus, Jay was there, a full-time dad and a supportive one. We both dropped out of school to care for our son.

By now, Mom had started lashing out at me again, only it was emotional abuse this time. She called me every vulgar name you could call a woman: I was every kind of slut, whore, and whatever else you called someone to insult her. Maybe she was called those same names by her stepdad when she had become a sixteen-year-old mother herself. These fits of rage occurred regularly after CeQuan was born, sometimes right in front of Jay. It often crushed my spirits and made me cry. Jay held his peace toward her for as long as he could.

Before long, I was overwhelmed with Mom's rage and the stress of being a new mother. One day I broke down and cried and cried. I couldn't stop. Seeing me in my distress made Jay angry. He went into the hallway to speak with my mom. She hadn't stopped screaming.

"Alright now, Ms. Jay. That's enough. You got Kee in there crying because of what you're saying to her."

She continued, becoming even more harsh in her insults. It infuriated Jay.

He got up and walked out of our room into hers, again. "I told you that's enough!" he said with raised voice. "You got her in there crying. Why don't you just chill? What wrong with you?"

"Screw you, nigga," she said and spit on Jay.

I then heard a moment of silence. Moments later, Jay returned to our room with a scared look on his face.

"What's wrong, Jay?"

He didn't respond.

"Jay?"

He looked at me and said, "I punched her in the face."

I was shocked. I rolled off the bed and hurried into her room. She was stretched out on her bed, eyes closed. I walked over to her and talked to her. "Ma? Hey, ma?"

She opened her eyes weakly and reached out her hand, signaling me to help her. I grabbed her hand and pulled her up. As soon as she sat up blood started oozing down her face. Jay hit her so hard that her right cheek under her eye split wide open. She was still dazed. She stood to her feet and I helped her to the bathroom.

"Oh my God!" she exclaimed, looking at herself in the mirror. I couldn't tell if she was dazed because she was drunk or because of the blow Jay just gave her. She wasn't drunk, though. She had just come back from one of her missions and needed rest.

Jay came to the bathroom door. He looked at the blood seeping from the gash under her eye, and he was visibly scared. "Let me take you to the hospital," Jay said.

"No, I don't want to go to the hospital," she answered, wiping the blood from her face. "If I go to the hospital they're going to want to know what happened. And if I tell them what happened, they're going to want to know who did it. If I tell them you did it they're going to come and lock you up." She was surprisingly coherent. "I'm not trying to go through all of that. But I'm going to tell you how we can fix this."

"How?" Jay asked.

"Just give me a little something to take away the pain and we'll make it go away."

Unsure what else to do, Jay agreed. The remainder of the night we were up, and Jay fed her cocaine. No longer was her eye an issue. I guess she was getting what she wanted in the first place and that was enough for her.

More than a year later, we were still making good money, but our new nextdoor neighbor didn't appreciate all the traffic around here at night. Every chance she got she reported us to the rental office. We tried to tame the traffic, but we just could not stop the money. In hindsight, I realized we weren't respectful to our neighbor. Our failure to comply with the rules and regulations of the property management resulted in Ms. Jay's eviction notice soon after. I was seventeen and three months pregnant with Jay's second baby when we were given thirty days to move. Mom didn't have anywhere else to go. But Jay's mother said that CeQuan and I could live with Jay and his parents if we wanted to. That was the golden opportunity I had been waiting for—to finally part ways with Ms. Jay. It had been pure hell living with her. It was not my problem that she was getting evicted; as long as my baby and I had somewhere else to go, it was good riddance. I was going to live with who I considered my new parents. I don't think Jay's mother ever knew how much I appreciated what she had done for me. Getting evicted and moving away from Mom was the best thing that had happened to me up to that point.

There was one trouble, though. I had become a hustler, and the only way I knew how to make money was selling drugs. How would I continue doing that without Jay's parents' knowledge? One day it came to me. Jay's friends were always around, and they loved smoking weed. As long as they didn't smoke in the streets, there would be no trouble with the police. At least that's how Jay's mom felt. Selling weed became my new hustle. I got in contact with a home girl I went to school with and she put me in touch with her cousin. Her cousin's contacts sold weed in weight, and I invested in a couple pounds. This hustle was all mine. Jay wasn't a part of this one. I also expanded the enterprise—weed gave smokers the munchies and they'd spend crazy money on junk goodies at the store after they smoke, so why not put their money in my pocket? I began selling food.

I purchased all kinds of meats and breads to make club sandwiches. I also bought chicken wings, fish, and French fries. After my customers ate, they needed something to drink. So I bought sodas and chips. I would sell them a club sandwich and fries with a drink for ten dollars. I also did the same things with the fish and chicken. I was a hustler. Any way that I could make a dollar was music to my ears. Not only did I sell them food and weed, but I started having socials on the weekends at the house of one of Jay's neighbors who let me use her space. I offered everything plus liquor, which I also sold. They gambled using both cards and dice. I was cutting the card tables and the dice games as well. In exchange for the usage of her house, I brought a little cocaine to compensate our neighbor. I appreciated her giving me the chance to make thousands on just one weekend. I did that week after week, and the money was great.

Mom was out of my life, for now, and everything seemed to be going swimmingly. I had an adorable son, my love Jay was right by my side, we had money flowing in all the time, and we were giddy with joy for our second child on the way.

CHAPTER 6

GOODBYE TO JAY

BEFORE MY SECOND PREGNANCY WAS OVER, THINGS BEGAN TO change. While we were financially more comfortable than ever before, Jay became restless. He took on a new interest, which turned into straight-out cheating while I was pregnant and stressed out with the move and expanding our money-making schemes. The woman was eleven years older than me. Surely, I couldn't compete. She was old and more experienced. I found comfort in crying myself to sleep at night, frustrated with the knowledge that Jay, my everything, was with another woman. He became bolder with his disrespect, allowing the other woman to pop up at our place out of the blue. Sometimes I was on the porch with Jay and his friends when she pulled up. Every time, he'd get right in the car with her and leave, in front of my face, as if I was nothing to him.

I had to cope with it somehow, and I turned to smoking weed even while I was pregnant. I began to hate Jay, and I made a promise to myself that he was going to pay for every moment of hurt and pain he caused me while I was pregnant.

On May 27, 1996, I gave birth to my baby. I named him Ketwan. He was seven pounds and twelve ounces, bigger than CeQuan at birth. He looked just like Jay, only cuter.

Unlike with my first birth, Jay was nowhere to be found when I welcomed Ketwan to the world. It seemed as though as the due date approached, he stayed away more and more. I was sure it was that older lady who deliberately kept him away from us out of jealousy. Where Jay and my own mother lacked, Jay's parents more than made up for. They were there always, in every way imaginable, and I appreciated it.

When I came home with Ketwan from the hospital, Jay's mother told me he had been incarcerated. She said me if I wanted to we could take the baby to see his dad at the city jail. I agreed. I wanted to see him. I needed to know what was so important that would make him miss the birth of our child. But more than anything, I needed him to see his son, who looked so much like him.

To my surprise, when we arrived at the jail, his old lady was there. Seeing her infuriated me. It wasn't enough for her that I suffered through my pregnancy. She made sure that I knew she was there and wasn't going anywhere. Suddenly I didn't have much to say to Jay, who sat on the other side of a thick slab of glass and was speaking to me over the jail phone. He had the biggest smile when I held up Ketwan for him to have a good look at. I caught the old lady watching my son trying to see if he looked anything like his dad. Jay told me she tried to convince him that Ketwan wasn't his, as if she would know where I spent my nights! I hoped she got a good look. Jay couldn't deny our son if he wanted to. He was definitely his father's child.

Now that I was no longer pregnant, I got busy with losing weight to get my body back. It was now payback time, as promised. Nothing good ever comes of spite. But I was young and I needed to hurt Jay the way he hurt me to show him how it felt. At the same time, I was constantly applying for apartments to get my own crib. Jay had been splitting his time between the old lady and me, and I had had enough of that. Two weeks after I turned eighteen, my first apartment came through. I was happy—it was time to serve up vengeance.

My hustle followed me right to my new crib. I moved not far from Fulton Hill, where Jay lived, to some apartments a few miles away called Hilltop. I hated it—it was old, ugly, and not far from the city dump. For the time being, though, it meant I could leave Jay behind.

When I moved out, I gave the old lady the clown she so badly wanted. She stayed by his side, acting as though she had "won." But as far as I was concerned, I was the winner and she the loser. Despite her age, she didn't have sense enough to see the reality of the situation. What good does it do to win over a piece of good-for-nothing? I was done with Jay and I moved on.

With Jay's agreement, I kept his Jeep and brought it to my new crib.

My brother Biggs had gotten in touch with me around this time and moved in. He was a big help with his nephews and whatever else I needed his help with. He would even tell me which guys were interested in me. I wasn't too eager to meet them, because I was very particular about who I wanted. If he wasn't it, he wasn't for me. Biggs knew that about me but still insisted on this one guy, and he pestered me every day. Finally, he confessed and said the guy paid him well to hook us up. The mystery man was also a hustler, just as I was—except he had way more than I did. I wasn't impressed; I had money, more than enough for my family and then some, so it'd take much more to get me interested.

I left home early one day to run errands. When I got back, Biggs was sitting outside across the parking lot, talking to one of his friends. There was a new one I hadn't seen before. When I got out of the car Biggs called out to me. "Kee, hold up!"

I paused and turned around, watching him walk up to me.

"Remember the dude Lil T I've been telling you about? That's him right there." He pointed to the guy sitting on the car, who he was talking to when I pulled in.

"Ewww!" I said. Lil T waved at me but I didn't wave back. I turned and starting walking toward my door.

Biggs repeated after me, "Eww? Eww what? You tripping."

"First, he's light-skinned and you know I don't do light-skinned. Second, he's skinny, and I hate that."

Before I aired the rest of my complaints, Biggs cut me off. "He's skinny. So what? Feed that fool then. Dude is full up."

"So? I got my own money."

"Yeah, you got your own money, but not like him."

"Whatever." I shook my head and walked in the house.

A few days passed with me carrying on buying weed, selling weed, and hosting weekend socials. Jay's homeboys continued to show love even though he and I were no longer a couple. They came to every social I hosted, bought my weed, smoked here, ate, gambled, and reported back to Jay everything that was going on at my house because he wasn't allowed there. When he wanted to see his boys, I took them to his parents' place. I was done with him and I wasn't about to send mix signals.

Biggs wouldn't stop going on about Lil T, though. "Just give the dude a chance," he'd say.

So he was persistent, plus being loaded. It still wasn't enough. He was getting to me through my brother; did it mean he was too much of a coward to approach me directly? Eventually, he did approach me.

One afternoon I came back home from the store, and on my way into my apartment when Lil T materialized out of nowhere.

"Hi, Miss Keisha. How are you doing?" he began. "Look, I know your brother has been telling you that I've been trying to holler at you for some time now."

"*And?*" I pursed my lips, not hiding my impatience with where he was going with this conversation.

He smiled and said, "Look, I can take care of you. What do you want? Name it and I got you." At that, he started pulling out huge knots of rubber band-wrapped money from all of his pockets.

Wow, now this was different. I had money, but, like Biggs said, not *this* kind of money. I was impressed for sure. It seemed only fair that I gave Lil T a shot. I wanted to know how he got so successful.

We grew close very fast. He bought me all kinds of things and helped me with bills. All the while, Jay's boys still came, buying weed from me and showing me tons of loyalty and love. Before long, Lil T moved in and I gave him a key. He deserved it. He was doing things for me that he didn't have to, and without me asking. Jay's boys saw Lil T at my place all the time and reported it all to Jay. I didn't care. Jay was nothing more to me than my boys' dad.

I walked to the corner store one day just up the hill when Jay decided to pay a visit. Lil T and Biggs were home with the boys, and Jay had met Lil T. On my way home, Jay was leaving in his dad's van, and jumped out when he saw me.

"Who is that dude in your house?"

The nerve of him. Was he here to interrogate me? I told him it was none of his business who I had in my own house. He said anyone hanging around his boys was his business. I saw right through the thin argument; it was just his way of trying to control me. Failing at engaging me, he returned to his dad's van, but not before asking if he could come spend some time with the boys.

I laughed, knowing he was finding an excuse to get a look of Lil T. "No, you can't come to my house. If you want to spend time with the boys, you can get them right now or I'll bring them to your parents' place."

"Whatever, I'll be back tonight." He jumped in his dad's vehicle and pulled away.

Later that night, the kids were sleep and Lil T and I were in bed. Around midnight, when I got up to use the bathroom, I heard a knock on the front door before I walked out of the bedroom. I thought it was someone for Biggs, whom wasn't there at the time. I turned around and said to Lil T, "Let them knock, whoever it is. I'm not answering that door." I turned back around and headed toward the bathroom, which was located directly across the hall. After I took another step out of the bedroom door, there was another quick knock and then silence. I paused again before entering the hallway. Then I heard someone coming up my stairs.

I turned to look, and it was Jay. "Oh my God, boy!" I was startled. "How'd you get in here? Who let you in my house?" I asked, while shutting my bedroom door at the same time.

"Don't worry about it. Who's in there?" Jay said as he pushed me aside and opened the bedroom door. He said to T, "Come on cuz, you got to get out of here."

I followed Jay into the bedroom and saw Lil T standing there fully dressed. My alarm when he heard me speak must've warned him to prepare himself.

"Nigga, your're crazy. I ain't going nowhere," Lil T replied.

"You're getting out of here. This is my baby mother's crib."

"So nigga, this is my girl, and I ain't going nowhere. Better yet, you want me gone, nigga, put me out."

I looked around and saw all of Jay's boys had come up my stairs and were standing in my bedroom. It was about fifteen of them.

They shoved me out of my bedroom, saying "We just want to talk to him real quick. We're not going to do anything to him." They shut and locked my bedroom door.

The next several minutes I was in a panic. I was scared for Lil T. He was out numbered and I had no idea what they were going to do to him. After a few minutes the door opened and they were walking behind Lil T. I was bewildered—who the hell did they think they were, coming in my house and causing all this commotion? They saw Lil T off through the cut and I followed them.

I knew exactly where he was headed so I yelled, "I'll be over there in a minute!"

Jay stood right in front of me while I watched T disappear. All of his boys piled in his dad's big old-school van. He started crying in front of me, having witnessed my concern for my new boo. "I can't believe you did this to me. Then you're going to stand right here and act like you care about that nigga. You're worried about that dude like you love him or something."

He looked beyond pathetic. I wanted so badly to laugh and to tell him it served him right to stand there with hurt feelings and tears. He deserved that for giving me the same hurt feelings when I was pregnant with *his* child. Checkmate! But I kept quiet. The payback was enough. He continued to pour out his heart, but I felt no sympathy for him. The smirk on my face told it all—he meant nothing to me.

After they left, I went to Lil T's cousin's house and got him. We went back to my home as though nothing had happened. But things didn't last too much longer between Lil T and me after that. A new apartment had come through for me around the Southside of Richmond and I was eager to move. Quickly, I packed my things and my children and I never looked back.

CHAPTER 7

NEW YORK STINTS

In our new neck of woods, although also in the Southside of Richmond, I had to find new ways around. Ruffin Road Apartments were spacious, nice and clean, and mixed with a little bit of hood. I liked it there, but I put my hustling on hold for just a little while as I scouted out the area and the people.

Within weeks, I befriended a couple of people. I was never too fond of being around a whole lot of chicks because usually my mindset was different from theirs. I was always a hustler, but the usual women I met had their minds set on other things. For this reason, I was a loner, but I never felt the need to be validated. I didn't need girls to help me know myself or to make me stand out. I stood tall, alone. Even Sonja was no longer around. It had been years since I saw her last. She got lost somewhere in between my moves.

This new chick Mandy I met around Ruffin Road was cool. We clicked right away and our friendship deepened the more time we spent around each other. She started going with me to Fulton Hill to have smoke sessions and chill times with Jay and his friends. We ran into a guy while leaving Jay's one day. He sat at the bus stop where we caught our bus. He listened to us talk for a minute and introduced himself.

"Hello ladies. I'm Cuban. Where are y'all headed?"

We recognized the New York accent right away. I was hesitant to start a conversation with this eager stranger. "We're going home," I responded coolly.

Mandy laughed, seeing the concerned look on my face. She was goofy like that, plus she was still feeling the effects of the weed. We both were.

"Oh okay. Where were you ladies just coming from?"

"Why?" I shot back.

"You're feisty, miss! Calm down. I was just asking, that's all," he said with a smile on his face.

"If you must know, we're just leaving my baby daddy's crib. Any more questions?"

"Yeah. Aren't you ladies going to introduce yourselves?"

"For what? We don't know you."

Mandy continued to giggle, leaving me to do the heavy lifting in this uninvited conversation.

"Well, I'm trying to get to know you ladies. That's why I'm talking to you, but you're being difficult."

At that, I turned down a notch. "Well, my name is Keisha and that's Mandy."

"Hey Mandy, do you talk? Because I see you've been over there giggling the whole time I've been talking to your friend here."

"What do I need to talk for? She's answering your questions," Mandy said.

From there, the conversation took a sharp turn that neither of us anticipated.

"You girls want to make some money?"

I got offended right away. "What do you mean do we want to make some money?" I wasn't sure what he was suggesting, and I didn't like the suspense of his approach.

"Calm down. Let me explain," he said. "My people and I are from New York and we got a little transportation business we're running." He shifted his gaze from me to Mandy, and back to me, with a mysterious look hinting at something that he thought would have our interest. "If you girls are down, you both could be a part of the business and we'd all make money together. Just under one condition: you'd both have to go to New York."

Mandy and I looked at each other.

"What do you ladies think?"

"I love the sound of money. You're talking my language. I'm down," I said to Cuban.

"That's what's up. Me too," Mandy chimed in.

"Alright!" he said, smiling. "That's what's up. I need both you ladies' phone numbers so I can call you later. That way we can get better acquainted."

"You can reach me at her house. I stay with her," Mandy told Cuban.

Just as I was giving him my phone number, the bus pulled up and we parted ways. The next day I got a call from Cuban.

"Yo, is this Keisha?" the voice on the other end of the phone asked.

"Yes. This is she. Hey you." I already recognized his voice.

He was straight to the point. "Yo, is it cool if I come by your crib so we could go into further detail about the business we spoke about yesterday?"

"Yeah, that's cool." I gave him my address, and an hour later Cuban was at my door.

Mandy, Cuban, and I sat down and chopped it up. He explained in depth about the drug transporting business we signed up for. Having learned exactly what we were going to be doing, I wasn't deterred from my new gig, although it meant a possibility of doing time if we were caught. Almost immediately, Mandy and I took our first trip.

Back then, Lil Kim was fresh on the scene. She was provocative and enticing with her clothing and in her "get money" lyrics. Her music energized me. I dug her so much that I was inspired to dye my hair with one of her signature colors, platinum blond, and it had become my signature. I stood out. I was different. And I made sure that my boys also not only lacked for nothing but also stood out among their peers. Their needs were all provided for, and they never missed doctor's appointments. I was on top of my game, but I was ready to climb even higher.

The money from transporting started off okay. But I had gotten bored with my pay and needed more. Mandy's hustle was short-lived—she quit after just a few trips. Her paranoia about getting caught got the best of her. Not me though. There was no way I was stopping. I kept going, transporting twice as much as before.

While I continued the transporting, I thought of ways to get things popping in my new hood. Everywhere I lived I was successful at bringing in money by selling drugs, and I was sure I could do it at Ruffin Road too. All I needed was product. I had an idea, and I wasted no time in calling up Cuban to tell him about my plan.

"Yo!" He answered the phone within three rings.

"Listen, Cuban. I want to run something by you and see what you think of it."

"Go ahead. Shoot."

I proposed that he would be my new go-to guy for the product I needed. He could even possibly pay me in cocaine instead of cash for my transporting runs, or half in cash and half in product.

"Are you serious?" he sounded surprised.

"Yes, I'm serious."

"I had no idea you'd be putting down the work," he said. "But if that's what you want, we can definitely do that."

"That's what's up!" I said, grinning from ear to ear.

Before we hung up, Cuban told me that in a couple of days he needed me to shoot back up top. I told him that was no problem. I was there whenever he needed me.

"Cool, I'm going to hit you up tomorrow, ma," he said. And we hung up.

The next day, Cuban popped up at my door. He didn't even call like he said he would. I didn't mind though. When I saw him, I saw my money, and I didn't care how he delivered the money, phone call or not. He came over just to tell me that I was leaving for New York the next morning and to give me my train ticket. I arranged for babysitting for my sons and was off to New York. My trip lasted only a brief two days. The second night I was already back in Virginia and took a cab straight to Cuban's spot, loaded with cocaine and anticipating my pay. I told him I wanted all work, no cash.

After he finished counting and weighing what I just bought in, he dropped more work on the scale and bagged all that he dropped. I had no idea he was about to hand me all the product he just bagged. But he did, and I was like a kid trick-or-treating with a bag full of goodies. I did not expect what he was giving me. My eyes saw money and I was excited to get home.

"I'm home!" I said shutting and locking the door behind me. The boys were asleep and out came my mother, smiling and greeting me.

After we moved to Ruffin Road, I ran into my mother and saw that she was no longer the evil witch she was when I saw her last. She was different, but her condition was no different—still impoverished, still addicted. She continued to pop in and out of my life after we ran into each other, but generally she helped me out a lot whenever I needed someone to watch the boys.

"Hey ma," I said to her. "I got something I want you to try."

That put a big smile on her face. "Oh yeah. What's that and where is it?" she looked like a five-year-old on the morning of her birthday, ready to open her presents.

"Hold on for a minute."

I walked in the kitchen and got a plate. I grabbed the new pack of razors and the scale I bought right before I left. Bringing it all back to my room, I shut and locked the door and got to work. I dumped the contents of the bag of coke onto the plate. I cut a .6 piece for Mom as appreciation for looking out for my kids whenever I needed her. When I was ready to present her little treat, I opened my door and called her to my room. I put the coke in her hand and asked her to let me know how it was after she was done. She smiled looking at the treat in her hand; it meant more to her than the money I'd usually give her. She quickly went into my bathroom to try it out and I went straight upstairs to my nosey neighbor's house to kick-start her also. l. My instructions to her were the same as the ones I had given my mom.

"Let me know how it is when you're done." I knew exactly what I was doing. Besides wanting to know the true quality of the product, my money-making would begin with them. They would be my word-of-mouth campaign in this new gig. After about twenty minutes or so, my mom came out of the bathroom.

"That is some good stuff, Kee." Before she could say more, there was a knock on the door.

"Hold on, ma." I walked over to the door while yelling, "Who is it?"

"It's me, Allison," my nosey neighbor said from the other end of the door.

As soon as I opened the door, she hurried inside. "Girl, that is some good stuff you gave me. Where you get that from? Do you have some more? If you do I got twenty dollars." She dropped it all on me without making eye contact once. She didn't pause either to let me answer any of her questions. She was high.

I could tell the coke was good even if she or my mom hadn't said anything. Their body language and behavior told it all. I knew how people reacted when they smoked good coke. I was pleased to see their response as proof that I had good product. I was taught to buy only good product because that was what built the clientele and kept them coming back.

"Please tell me you got some more of that good stuff," Allison repeated.

"Yes ma'am, I surely do. It's a lot more where that came from," I said.

"Let me get a twenty," she asked.

I went into my room and came back dropping in her hand a piece that was already weighed and bagged.

"All of this for twenty dollars?"

"Yes ma'am. Those are .5, scale weighed and they go for twenty. I don't sell nothing less than that so don't come with less than twenty or I can't do nothing for you."

"Oh my God, thank you!" she said, reaching for the door, impatient to go home and get these treats into her system.

That night I went from two customers to twenty. Word traveled fast about that fire I was selling and how I gave them double of what their money paid for. My method afforded me to lock down any place I started selling at. Soon, I had the whole neighborhood and a big part of the south on lock. I kept good product and I never switched up my tactic. Neither did I worry about giving away too much of it. In my eyes it was always better for it to sell itself quicker, than to hold on to it because no one wanted to buy it. It went so fast that I didn't miss what I gave away. I wasn't one of those street corner dealers. I was a hustler. There's a difference. I didn't have to chase down cars and sell to different strangers all day. Once my people bought from me, they would never spend money anywhere else. I made sure of that. I took care of them. I even looked out for my faithful people when they didn't have money to spend. For those reasons, I didn't have to sell my product. It sold itself. I never had to compete, because there was no competition.

The street dealers didn't get it. They wasted their time trying to beat people for their money, selling any type of product because it didn't matter to them. They never realized that quality trumps quantity, and they wondered why their business never grew, why they remained street dealers buying the same quantity of drugs year after year.

I kept buying my product from Cuban and continued transporting as well. I learned that it was better to have more than one way of income because you never know what might happen if one crashes.

My trips to New York had been successful and were becoming more frequent, three maybe four times a week. Cuban asked if I knew of anyone else I could put down so I wouldn't have to travel alone. I told him the truth—I had no other reliable source I could trust in that way. I continued my solo trips to NY and began attracting unwanted attention. It certainly didn't help that my hair was platinum blond. You couldn't miss me even in a New York City crowd.

I had been doing the trips without problems for a few months. Cuban got Mandy and me started in the summertime, and now it was in the thick of the winter, with snow piled up high on the streets of both Richmond and New York. This wintry day, I was stopped in my tracks after getting off the train in Richmond. I was headed for the taxi when the gentlemen approached me.

"Excuse me, ma'am," a plainclothes man of average height and stocky build addressed me. "We've been noticing you a lot around here lately because of your hair. You travel quite frequently, miss." He paused. "I'm sorry, what's your name?"

I immediately put up my guard but answered his question. "I'm Chantel," I said, scanning both of them from head to toe.

"Like I was saying, Miss Chantel," continued the man, scratching his balding head now and then, "we've been noticing you a lot lately and we have reason to suspect you're involved in illegal activity."

They both pulled out their badges. The other one, a tall man with a mustache, said, "We're cops working with the narcotics department of

Virginia. We have reason to believe that you've been trafficking drugs. Is it too much to ask if we may check your things?"

I was thrown off, though not completely. Cuban had trained Mandy and me for situations like this. I remained calm, although in my stomach I had the bubble guts. Had I shown any fear or acted guilty, they probably would've called the dogs and that would've been it for me. "Sure, I don't mind," I said coolly.

"Great. And your coat, too, please," the half-bald man said while the taller officer took my things from my hand and began his search. "I just have a couple questions for you," the officer continued.

"Okay," I said politely, suddenly filled with a surge of confidence. My life was on the line. I had to play it cool. There was nothing in my bag; all the drugs were loaded inside the lining of my fur coat. As long as they didn't get the dogs out here, there was no way a regular pat-down by these two guys could result in anything. I just needed to keep cool.

"First, are you involved in any kind of drug activity?" he asked.

I smiled. Are you kidding me, I thought. What a stupid question. Would anyone ever say yes to that question?

"Drug activity, me? No, absolutely not," I denied.

"Well, why do you travel so much? Who are you coming and going to see so frequently?"

"I live here, officer. But my boyfriend lives in DC. We both travel frequently to see each other until we work out which of us will move in with the other. He has his own place and I have mine."

"Uh huh, I see," the half-bald officer said. By this time, the search turned up dry.

The taller officer said, "We're clear. She doesn't have anything," and handed my bags and coat to me.

That was the best news my ears had heard in a long time.

"Okay," the stocky officer turned to me. "Well, thank you for your cooperation. And we're sorry to have bothered you at all. Here are your things. You're free to go."

I smiled and thanked them both. Then I grabbed my bags and walked over to the queue of taxis in front of the train station. "Oh my God, oh my God," I whispered under my breath as my heart continued pounding.

I climbed into the backseat of the nearest cab and gave him the address to Cuban's spot. I had enough cocaine on me that if they had sent the dogs, the judge would've thrown the book at me. Thank God the dogs weren't involved. This was definitely the end of my career as a transporter. That was way too close.

At Cuban's, I told him what happened and was resolute in my decision that this was my last time. The pay for my trips wasn't enough to have years of my life snatched away from me on account of someone else. If I was going to be doing any jail time at all, it would be for my own self.

Cuban tried to convince me to continue making trips. He even suggested that I change my hair. He didn't care about the risks I faced. Making money was his priority, and I understood that. In the street life every man is for himself. You only care about those who are near and dear to you. Everybody else means nothing. And that was the relationship I had with Cuban. We benefited each other tremendously. But I didn't care about him. Neither did he care about me. That's why he insisted that I continue making trips, even offering to pay me double. It sounded good. Still, it wasn't enough for me. I asked him for my final pay all in work. But I insisted that I'd never transport again. Thus ended my nine-month stint as a transporter.

CHAPTER 8

FULL-TIME IN THE GAME AT RUFFIN ROAD

Although I no longer transported for Cuban, we stayed in touch because he was my go-to man to buy my weight. Every now and again, he tried to convince me to go back to work. But I stood my ground. That gig was over.

My life in the drug game continued forward full-force. I was put on with a new drug connect through my people. My new guy had some serious fire, even better than the product I got from Cuban. This stuff from Jamaica was raw and pure. My customers went crazy over it and my clientele steadily grew. Those street corner dealers looked on with jealousy because my hustle emptied their pockets for the most part. They started hanging in my hallways and filling the entire staircase of my building, threatening my customers out of desperation. But nobody took them seriously. After all, it was their money and nobody could force them to buy something they didn't want.

I was asked several times by some of the neighborhood knuckleheads to sell them weight. I declined. I wouldn't do it even though I could. Flat-footing my drugs made more sense to me. Plus, I had the best drugs around there. I wasn't about to allow the competitors to try and compete. I loved being in a class all by myself. In the process, I made quite a few enemies unintentionally. But I didn't show any fear. I only went out and purchased street protection to protect my family and me.

By now Mandy was completely out of the picture. Sonja and I found each other and she was back in my life full force again. I missed her. I still considered her my best friend. And just as I stayed loyal in my affections for Sonja, Mom held on to her misgivings as when she used to warn me that Sonja wasn't a true friend. I brushed Mom off—how could I respect any advice from a junkie? To me, Sonja was my best friend. She never gave me any reason not to trust her.

As my hustle continued and expanded, my crib became the heart of my people. My brother Biggs and his girl were there almost every day. Aunt Janice also moved to a place only a few blocks down the street from me. Mom was staying with me. And our cousin Craig was always there since the other side of his family lived in Ruffin Rd. I gave Craig and Biggs keys to my crib. They were welcomed to come and go as they pleased.

Biggs was still my baby. He looked up to me and I babied him. Whatever he knew, he learned from watching either me or Jay. But for years I had been his only example. Neither of our dads had been consistent in our lives. The streets trained me, and I trained my brother. I gave him the streets like I gave it to Sonja. And I looked out for them both. I looked out for cuz too, with crazy product for a little bit of nothing to help him get on. I was a female Scarface with blond hair, loved by both family and customers.

Both my mom and my aunt carried on the way they used to when I was growing up, spending all the money they had—and the money they didn't have—on drugs and getting high together. I didn't care though. Janice was still my aunt. And Mom was still Mom. I no longer saw Mom as unrespectable; I had accepted who she'd become. Also, it helped to be apart from her for a few years. The tension was relaxed, and I was ready to have her back in my life regularly.

Every now and then, I hung out with a couple of girls I went to school with. We didn't have many heart-to-heart talks, but we knew how to have fun together, especially Jeanette. She called me up when her twenty-first birthday was coming up and invited me to her weekend trip to Virginia Beach for her birthday. She invited a few other chicks as well. We made plans together and split the cost of a big suite. I was all for it. I had never been to the beach. I was so stoked that even the preparation was exciting. We couldn't get over the hype that someone amongst us was turning twenty-one and could legally go into the alcohol store. We went in all together and picked out the alcohol we wanted. We gave Jeanette the money to buy all the alcohol for the group.

Part of my preparation was shopping for my beach attire and heels at a lingerie store. I never put a limit on any of my clothing purchases and this was no different. I had it going on and it showed by the way I dressed. I carried myself with confidence. With a fresh twenty-two-inch blond wet-n-wavy hair-do, heels, and sexy party clothes for the weekend, I was ready to have the time of my life.

Our first night in the suite was laid back. We all put on regular swimsuits and went to the hotel's swimming pool. With drinks in our hands, we were grown and sexy young women ready to have a good time. I wasn't putting myself out casually, though. I held to my standards, not talking to just any guy that tried to strike up a conversation. At the pool we met some guys visiting from a different state. They gave us fliers inviting us to a party the following evening. We accepted their invitation. We laughed, talked, and flirted the night away with them. Soon it was almost 3:00 a.m. We said our good nights to the gentlemen and turned in for the night.

Early the next morning, even with just about four hours of sleep, we woke up without an alarm clock because of the sunlight that lit up our room. We prepared ourselves and took the elevator down to the lobby for the complimentary breakfast. Over orange juice, waffles, and breakfast sausages, we discussed and settled on our plans for the day. We giggled when we talked about the beachfront night party that we were invited to.

* * *

THE MUSIC OF Lil Cease and Lil Kim was turned on full blast on the boardwalk while we stepped on the scene. It was packed, with people of all races and sizes. Single men. Groups of hot ladies. Families with their children. There were car clubs riding in groups one after another. There were motorcycle gangs too. Everywhere I turned my eyes there was a sight to see. The entire boardwalk was alive and popping. We walked down the boardwalk in swimsuits and heels as if we were on a runway, catching attention from every angle. My hair always made me stand out in crowds. Fellas were digging the platinum blond. Silently, the ladies were too but they expressed it in jealous hate. I caught stares from everybody. Even white men asked as I walked past them, "Is it true that blonds have more fun?"

We hadn't even set foot on the beach that entire day, since we were going to be there for the night party. We spent our day snacking, having midday cocktails on the boardwalk, checked out little charming shops—everything but walking on beach sand. Then at night, we changed into our showstopper outfits. Everyone saved their best for the last activity of the day, and I did the same. Jeanette had a banging body, and she had a stride that drew double-takes when she walked by. She and I always competed in who wore the better outfit. Hers was always more skanky, showing way more skin. Mine, though, was always more tasteful, more expensive. I was heavy on name brands, letting my attire attest to the fact that I had money and I wasn't a force to be reckoned with.

The party was right on the beach, at the end of a long stretch of soft sand. A few feet away from where the most of the crowd was sat a beach house, and we walked over to see what the partiers were up to there. Music was played loudly also in the extra-large room we stepped inside of. The security at the door checked us before allowing us to enter. The smell of alcohol and marijuana filled the air. The room was dark but we were able to maneuver through the crowd. Women danced provocatively, enticing the fellas who watched with lustful eyes. We girls stayed one another's heels, holding each other's hands as we moved across the dance floor. We finally made it to the alcohol stand, where we each got drinks to unwind.

Refreshed by our drinks, we began to dance the night away. We had a great time, although I kept my guard up. I scanned the place for Mr. Right, not just there but the entire time we were at the beach. I was ready for a man. Not just any man, but someone I could call my own. Someone who was on my level mentally. Someone I could build a life with. Had I met him there, it could've been the beginning of something beautiful. But that night, I never met him.

The party ended at 3:00 a.m. We had a blast the entire night and we fell asleep on much girl talk.

Sunday morning rolled around quickly, it was time to check out of our hotel. We took turns showering and packing, getting ready for the road trip back home. We stopped for breakfast right before we hit the highway because we missed the hotel breakfast. We reminisced the fun of the weekend and already began making plans for our next trip. The ride back home was smooth sailing, except my mind was laser-focused on what I had blown over the weekend. The girls laughed and talked while I sat quietly counting and recounting my money in my head. I was obsessed with making money, but I didn't care for spending it. "Oh well," I thought, "I'll just have to make up for it when I get home." I put the money worries out of my mind and joined in the girls' chatter for the remainder of the ride.

Back home, my customers missed me over the weekend and when they saw me back, they showed me mad love. I missed them too. I made so much money that night that it tripled what I'd spent over the weekend. I was glad to have the money, because very soon I'd have to splurge—my eldest son, CeQuan, was turning five. His birthday only five days after mine, I planned several months ahead to make sure it would be a memorable double celebration for all of us.

Besides pampering my children on their birthdays and making sure I dressed in clothing that reflected my worth, I was not reckless with money. My mission was staying out of the poverty that I had become so accustomed to growing up. In our abject poverty, I had nothing to look forward to except a rescuer to come from nowhere and deliver me. I had no dreams, no aspirations. Now that I was a young adult, capable of bringing in money of my own, I would not allow anything to happen to us that would make my boys experience what I did as a child. I was going to be the best mother I knew how. My children would not live in poverty, and I made sure to give them anything they wanted or needed. Gone were tattered clothes and empty refrigerator. Now I had fast money, and my boys would never be ashamed the way I was.

The first week of October came faster than I expected, but I was ready for the big occasion. CeQuan's happiness meant my happiness, and I spent the greater part of the first two weeks of October making preparations for his birthday party. On the day of CeQuan's birthday, I had Jay pick him up and spend time elsewhere while I prepared our place for the party. I made sure not to miss any details, from birthday cake, balloons, and decorations, to piñata, food, gifts, games. I had them all, and I invited tons of friends and kids to fill the house. When we were all ready for CeQuan, I called Jay and told him to bring the birthday boy home.

"Surprise! Happy birthday!" everyone yelled in unison when CeQuan walked in. The sweet smile on his face was priceless. I teared up as I captured those moments on camera—my baby had turned five. Where did all the time go? There was no time for these thoughts, though, CeQuan busied himself opening the gifts and the guests dived into the food and games. My son was happy, and that was worth the money I spent on the day.

My birthday was just five days earlier than his, and the only thing I had planned for my own birthday treat was an upcoming show I was interested in. A few weeks earlier, a man approached me when I was walking home one evening from my car. He offered tickets to the same show I wanted to go to, for a really great price. I bought two on the spot, for Sonja and me. But I remembered as I was cleaning up after CeQuan's party that I needed to get myself ready for the show. In less than a week I had to get my hair done and pick out my outfit.

I called up my stylist and made an appointment two days before the show. Sonja and I went shopping together afterwards, but it turned out rather unpleasant for me. Even though Sonja was my girl and she was used to me treating her, I didn't feel like buying her clothes this time—it was *my* birthday. Having to cover Sonja's expenses had grown tiresome for me. She wasn't my child, and I was tired of treating her as such. I told her if she didn't have money, she was welcomed to wear something from my closet to the show. It was a good offer, because I had a ton of clothes brand new or worn only once; many still had tags on.

For me, though, I was the birthday girl, and I painstakingly picked out the best outfit my money could buy from Cloverleaf Mall in Richmond. At the show, I sat in the front row, shining in my outfit and newly done hair like the star I was.

First up was Big Pun, who shouted into the mic, his broad voice reverberating through the hall from huge speakers as he tirelessly walked back and forth on the stage, singing and interacting with the audience. The crowd went crazy. Foxy Brown was up next with her sassy tone and revealing attire. She confidently swayed across the stage while rapping, followed by Jay Z and Amil.

The band rocked on, and the crowd swayed left and right, jumping up and down. It felt as though the energy of the place would tear open the roof above us. The rappers came back one after another, more pumped as the night went on, and the crowd roared. I don't think one booty touched the chairs of the theater that night. The show topped every other event I ever attended. Afterward, I dropped Sonja off at home and she thanked me before saying good night. The rest of the evening was quiet, spent with watching television on my own and making money whenever a customer came knocking on the door.

*　*　*

IT ALWAYS FELT like time accelerated after our October birthday's. Soon it was Thanksgiving. Like how it always was at Sister's, this year we made Thanksgiving a big occasion. I filled the house with family and friends. Some of my girlfriends from the neighborhood, like Allison and Mandy, brought their children. My brother and his girlfriend also came, along with Aunt Janice and all four of her children. My two boys and their father, Jay, were all there, although Jay didn't stay long.

My aunt and mom cooked whatever ingredients I provided them. I watched them cook while smoking and making money. Soon Mom and Aunt Janice brought out all kinds of dishes from the kitchen and filled the dining table and kitchen countertops: ham, chitterlings, pasta salad, tuna salad, potato salad, seafood salad, turkey, stuffing, gravy, yams, greens, and on and on.

After the cooking was done, the older adults fixed dinner plates for the children and entertained them. We younger adults went into my bedroom to get a smoke cypher going. After cyphering four blunts between five of us, we were somewhere in between the moon and the stars when we walked back into the kitchen to fix our plates. There were already six people sitting around the eight-seat dining table. We grabbed chairs to join them, laughing and giggling and talking nonsense the whole time. How weed made us all silly back then! Everything was funny after smoking a blunt.

At the table we did more laughing than eating. We laughed about Aunt Janice's coarse, short and nappy afro that never grew. About her son having the same texture and length of hair, except he didn't realize the joke was on him; he was only ten.

We had a great time that night. It was beautiful. Full of family, games, and fun times. Just like at Sister's when I was growing up. I longed for and missed those times. When I could, I tried with everything in me to emulate what I was shown as a child—that family was everything—and to always keep family around.

The day after was spent winding down and cleaning; that is, by Mom and Aunt Janice.

I was alone in my room, thinking about how much money I had spent for Thanksgiving, and how I'd have to plan for Christmas and other end-of-year expenses. I sat on my bed staring into the huge closet that my clothes filled. I counted my money and the product I had left. I realized I had to stop spending money. I was never reckless, but perhaps I had reason to cut back some—I had money, but it wasn't growing. Was all my hustle in vain? How would I make my money grow?

I began looking at where I spent money. I could stop going to the mall and stop going out to restaurants or clubs. The only things I couldn't let go of were my hair and nails. Everything else I could sacrifice until I figured out a better money-making scheme. I thought of how lovely it would be to become a kingpin, not hustling .5s from my place and making thousands of dollars daily doing so, but being the woman behind the scenes, the supplier of product for Richmond's streets. From that moment on, that was my goal: to become a kingpin.

With my saving mindset in place, I began to build my money quickly, and I was excited to be on my way to the top. I became so organized and laser-focused that I developed a system that helped me to stay on top of my money and work. I was still selling .5-mg bags, but it was only going to last till I bought my first kilo.

* * *

I WAS SITTING at the kitchen table looking through my two shoe boxes when Sonja came over. One of the boxes held money and the other product. I never waited until I was too low on product before I re-up. My stream of money was never-ending and that didn't make sense. I counted my money, putting it in stacks of thousands. Then I counted my work to know what my final numbers would be. I was satisfied. Sonja watched me in amazement. She had no idea what I was working with even though she saw I was constantly getting money.

"That's crazy," Sonja said, watching me like I had three eyes.

"What's crazy?"

"That you got money like that and I'm your best friend and I'm broke."

"What?" I had to stop what I was doing and looked up at her. I couldn't believe the words that came out her mouth. "What do you mean you're broke? Girl, as much as I look out for you, you shouldn't be. But if you are that's because you're trying to keep up with me." I couldn't hold back on that one. She needed to hear it.

I took her on shopping sprees whenever we went out, and I sold her tons of 500 packs of work for $50. She could've easily broken those down and doubled her money. The more I gave her, the more she expected from me, as if I were her husband or mother. It was time I stopped looking out for her. I was wasting my money trying to help her. With what I sold her for $50, I could have easily made a thousand dollars.

She was quiet. She knew it was truth, and she continued sitting in silence as she watched me finish going through the shoeboxes.

A few weeks later, Sonja came over with the plans of us riding through Maymount Park and downtown because those were the things to do on Sundays in Richmond. But she and I had to get high first. After cracking my blunt, I filled it with some of the big buds that were in the sandwich bag on the bed. I turned around and sat my blunt in the windowsill to break the weed before rolling it. After I was done, I turned back around to see Sonja sitting on the bed watching me. She had the nastiest look on her face. I ignored it and asked why she didn't roll her blunt.

With that same nasty look, she said, "You already rolled a blunt. Why should I roll one too?"

What was there to explain? We smoked together for heaven knows how many times, and there wasn't one single time we smoked that she and I didn't both roll up. Maybe she was still hurt by what I told her the other day in my kitchen.

"I can't stand you. You stupid walking pretty girl trick," she continued. The look on her face pierced me. Her eyes filled with such hatred, as if she wanted to do something to me.

"Stupid walking? What, girl, whatever." I brushed it all off. Surely, she was still upset about the other day, but she couldn't have meant it. I mean, it didn't even make sense. "Well, how about this," I said, "if you don't roll, you don't smoke. I guess I'll be smoking this all by myself." I sparked and started smoking my blunt, and Sonja began to roll hers.

After we finished smoking, we hopped in the car and took off, carrying on as if that awkward, unpleasant conversation didn't happen. In my mind, though, I couldn't help but replay her words. She called me a "stupid walking pretty girl trick." What did that even mean? I walked just like everyone else. Her strange remarks reminded me of how Mom told me when we were younger that Sonja wasn't truly my friend. Now I was beginning to see Mom must have said it for a reason I couldn't see. I started thinking of the money I was missing when I was riding out with her. But the ride was cool, and people were all over the place like every Sunday. Just as I was beginning to enjoy the ride, my pager went off.

"Sonja, stop me by this gas station real quick. I need to make a phone call."

"Alright," she said, pulling into the Exxon gas station.

I returned the phone call, knowing it was one of my sales. I was ready to go home after the call because my customers needed my product. As I walked back to the car from the phone booth, a car pulled in front of me. In it were two young men I hadn't met before. The driver was nice-looking but the one on the passenger side was some kind of fine.

"Excuse me, miss," the man in the passenger seat said to me. "Can I ask what's your name?"

I was thrown off by this comely face, but I steadied myself and returned a question before I'd answer his. "Why?"

"Why? I just want to know your name, that's all. Is that too much to ask, Miss Lady?"

I liked his response and told him my name was Keisha.

"Well, how are you doing, Miss Keisha? I'm Marcus and this is my boy Maurice," he said, pointing at the driver. "Do you have a boyfriend, Miss Keisha?"

He was straightforward, no-nonsense, and a gentleman. I liked him. I often questioned guys who tried to holler at me. Most times they'd get upset and show their true colors. What I found out was that if they were up to no good, they didn't like being questioned. Not Marcus, though. He was chill.

I told him I didn't have a boyfriend because I didn't want one. That was far from the truth, though. I was single because I refused to settle for anything less than my standard. The man of my choice had to reflect my worth and my standard—he should be good-looking and able to offer me a sense of security, and he should match my mentality in how I approached life, which was constant and consistent hustling. If I wasn't totally attracted to a guy, I wouldn't just roll with it. Even something as small as the yellow on a guy's teeth turned me off. I had firm standards. No guy was worth coming into my place and meeting my children unless we were serious. And if we weren't that serious, I didn't bother being just a random guy's fling.

For these reasons, I was alone and unimpressed by the countless guys that wanted to holler at me. I wasn't easily impressed, and much less by material things. I dug my own gold, and I made sure I—not someone else—took good care of my children. Lil T was not my type, but he was very persistent and that was why I gave him a try.

"Why?" he responded. "Why you don't have a man as good as you look?"

I gave him the tough girl look as if I was irritated. In reality, though, I wanted to just let loose with his fine self. But not just yet, I had to maintain my composure.

He giggled. "You're tough. I just was going to ask if I can get your number so I can call you."

"I'm sorry. But I don't just go around giving out my number. But you can give me yours and I might call you."

"Okay, I'll accept that. It's better than nothing."

He gave me his number and I took it and walked off. I wanted to have a girl moment and jump up and down the way girls do when they really like a guy and think he's hot. But I couldn't, at least not in his view. I got into the car and Sonja and I drove off.

Back at home, I ruminated again about what Sonja said. The only way I could make sense of her comment was that she meant I walked in a "stupid" manner. I needed to see what she saw. I grabbed my full-length mirror and brought it into the living room, setting it against the front door. I watched myself closely as I walked from the mirror and back toward it. I examined my every step. Sonja was right. My gait was more a stride than a walk. I walked away and toward the mirror several times, and I was shocked that I walked this way, as if I was on the runway. I had not noticed in all my twenty-one years of life, and I didn't even walk this way deliberately. I wouldn't even know how to change how I walked.

I thought of Marcus and decided to wait a few days before calling him. I had to maintain my tough girl act to show the cutie pie I wasn't like most girls, although I looked forward to seeing how things would unfold between us. It had been a long while since someone had my interest.

About five days after our first meeting at Exxon, I called up Marcus, and immediately we clicked. We had a great conversation, and it felt like we had known each other for years. After that, almost every day we were on the phone with each other. I was truly feeling that cutie pie, but I wouldn't let him know it. He had this bad boy image about himself. For me that meant protection and respect—he could protect me from the angry, jealous neighborhood dealers who had been threatening my safety—and that was something I definitely needed.

One month went by, then two. We got to know each other and we were in touch almost every day. One day, when I noticed he hadn't called, I thought nothing of it—maybe he was busy or just needed a break, which was cool with me. But one day stretched to two, four, six days. Something must have been going on, only I didn't know what. I had been visiting Marcus at Maurice's. Just as with other guys, I didn't easily allow just anyone to come to my place and meet my children. After two months of getting to know each other, I still hadn't told Marcus where I lived, other than somewhere on the Southside.

I decided that I'd show my face at Maurice's and find out what happened to Marcus. There, Maurice told me Marcus was incarcerated at the city jail. I wanted to know why, but I held my tongue because it was truly none of my business. Every so often I'd pop up at Maurice's to see if Marcus made it home.

By this time, Sonja had stopped coming around as often as before. I'd hear from her every other week or so. I think we both felt more distant from each other, and that was fine with me. There was no reason for me to throw away my hard-earned money to help someone who wasn't serious about working to keep the money. I loved her still, though. After all, she was with me through some very dark times earlier in my life. She was still my girl, but I scaled way back in looking out for her.

Four months after Marcus's disappearance, I visited Maurice one day, as I had been doing frequently, to check on Marcus. Each time I visited I hoped to see Marcus there, but when I actually found him there this day, I was surprised. Equal parts surprised and elated.

I knocked a few times on the door, and out came Marcus. He came out onto the porch and hugged me. I blushed like a thirteen-year-old meeting face to face with her school crush. He told me, looking into my eyes, that he missed me, and then he kissed my lips. I think I died and came back to life. I don't know what jail did to him but he was finer than before he left.

I shook my head a little to get back down to earth. Knowing by now some of the difficulties people face fresh out of jail, I asked if he needed money. He denied, but I sensed he didn't want to let me know the truth. Then I asked him if he wanted "work." He laughed. He hadn't known at that point what my business was, and he thought I was just joking.

"Where do you get work from?" He managed to spit out a question in between his laughs.

"What do you mean where I get work from? That's what I do."

"Are you serious?" He wasn't laughing anymore.

"As serious as a heart attack."

When he saw that I meant what I said, he said that he would take the work. I told him to give me a call the following day and I'd bring it to him. Then we caught up on each other's lives, new developments or lack thereof in the hood. Before I left, he kissed me goodbye and melted my heart a second time.

Marcus and I continued getting to know each other on the phone, and I'd come by Maurice's place to see him or bring him work. We learned a lot about each other and grew very close. We had not gone to bed with each other, but my guard had already been let down. I trusted him, and he liked me. He called me just as much as I called him, if not more. He was digging the sophisticated way I carried myself, which was rare among girls my age. Soon, he asked me on the phone to be his girl.

After it became official, I took him home with me right away. I introduced him to my mom and the boys. Then, when other family visited, one by one I introduced them all. Before Marcus met my family, he never mentioned his own to me, which was only natural. Shortly after meeting all of my family and seeing that we were no different from his relatives, he introduced me to his own mother.

Within a few weeks, Marcus moved in with my children and me. He immediately gave me a sense of security that I hadn't felt before. He was strong, respectful, and had a presence that commanded attention. I felt a natural respect for him that I didn't before with other men. But beneath the mean, tough, pit bull-like exterior, Marcus had a sweet side that he showed only to me.

A few days after Marcus moved into my crib, I felt it was time to lace my boo with a new wardrobe. It would take away from my savings goal, but he was worth it. Plus, as a couple, our style and fashion had to match at least when we went out in public. I found out what size clothing and shoes he wore. Early one morning while he was asleep, I got up, showered, dressed, and left for a day of wardrobe makeover for my man. I went downtown Richmond to a popping urban store named Cavaliers. That was where every guy that stayed fly shopped. Everything I felt he needed I got for him.

When I got home, the boys had woken up and were eating with mom in the kitchen. I said hi to them, kissed each of my sons on the forehead, and headed to my room. Marcus was there sitting on the edge of the bed when I walked in. He smiled and noticed the bags in my hands.

"Where have you been?" he asked.

I kneeled down between his legs and looked up into his eyes and kissed his lips. "Every single bag here is yours. I got them all for you. I noticed you needed more clothes, hon."

He smiled. "Thank you, sweets. You didn't have to." His voice was calm and sweet. It was just like the quiet joy we shared. We were both content and at peace in our relationship. There was no drama, no outbursts.

I grabbed all the bags and placed them in front of his feet. The same way I liked seeing my boys open gifts, I was excited to see him open those bags. "Here, go on. Try them!"

His smile got bigger and brighter as he went from bag to bag. I didn't miss anything. Polo shirts, jeans, Timberlands, undershirts. The most expensive popping brands in the hood at that time. Anything and everything he could've needed, I got for him. He meant more to me than he knew, and I wanted to show him how much I appreciated him. Not only was he sweet to me, he made me feel protected. I don't think there is any woman, young or old, who doesn't like to feel protected. And that was what he gave me. Protection.

I left Marcus to take a shower and get dressed while I went into the kitchen to fix him breakfast. By the time I returned to the bedroom, he was fully dressed and checking himself out in the mirror. I sat his food down on the night stand and walked over to him. He was just as fine as he wanted to be. And he was all mine. He pulled me into his arms and kissed me. Wrapping his arms around me, he thanked me again for his gifts. I could only blush while looking into the eyes of my man. I wished life would go on like this, with Marcus and me always together, always head over heels for each other.

After Marcus finished eating his breakfast, we smoked. He called up Maurice and agreed to go over to his place for a little while. I didn't mind. Just as long as he was coming back. Before he left, he kissed me again and told me he'd be back shortly. And I got to work.

Even though Marcus was living with me now, that didn't deter my clientele. In fact, the money seemed to pour in even more. Day and night, every day, all night. The volume of traffic around my crib became somewhat nerve-wracking and I had to start doing things differently. I came up with a cut-off time to keep my customers from banging my door down all night. It didn't work very well. When they saw both my vehicles in the parking lot, they knew I was home. They'd knock anyway; they wanted the drugs more than anything. If I didn't answer the front door, they knocked on my bedroom windows until I answered. But enough was enough, I had to put my feet down. If they wanted what only I could give them, they'd have to respect my game rules.

While I managed my growing business, I was still looking out for Marcus. When he ran out of work, I gave him more free of charge. I made sure he didn't have to leave the house to go hustle. I allowed him to dump his pack whenever he needed to. Before long, Marcus's boys Maurice and Rock started hanging at our spot. Every day they came by and chilled. I even allowed Maurice to sell his drugs at my crib too. My appreciation of Marcus and his friends made it no problem. Plus, Rock had done some things in the streets and built a reputation for himself as someone not to be messed with. They all were my security.

CHAPTER 9

"BOY" AND "GIRL"

SINCE I WAS THE GO-TO IN MY NECK OF WOODS FOR THE WORK, it was only natural that my customers started asking if I could offer other types of drugs, like heroin. That was never my thing. I didn't know anything about it. Neither had I ever considered selling it. But so many of my customers were cross-addicted and their growing requests made me reconsider. It seemed to make sense that two hustles were better than one, and I already had a strong clientele who preferred buying from me anyway. So, I called up my connect and asked if he knew where I could get some. Right away, he gave me the amount he thought I should start with.

From there, my second hustle was official; I knew exactly who I should tell first. Martha was married and lived in my hood. Both she and her husband were old-school dope heads, the kind that would pick your shirt up off your table and try to sell it to you as if you didn't know it was yours. But they were the perfect people to kick-start my product.

I went over to Martha's and knocked on her door.

"Hey girl. You have a minute to come over to my place?"

"Hey there." She had a spatula in her hand and an apron around her waist. "Something happened?"

"No, no. Just got something to show you. Got time now?"

I could tell Martha knew what I'd got for her. She said quickly, "Yeah. Just give me a second to finish frying my fish."

I left, smiling to myself. She'd be at my door within ten minutes, I knew it. Martha was the kind of person that couldn't resist good dope. Sure enough, I barely sat down on the sofa when she came knocking on the door. I let her in and, without saying a word, I gestured her over to the table and put a little brick in her hand. Her eyes sparked as if she was in the presence of her first love. She got up immediately and said she'd be back to tell me how it was.

If it were cocaine I could've easily sold it for twenty dollars. But I gave it to her for nothing. I didn't know what heroin was, how much it went for, and how it made people sick. I had absolutely no idea that once you get addicted to it, your body needed it. I knew hardly anything about my new hustle. But I didn't mind learning it if it meant money.

Within twenty minutes Martha was back in my kitchen. I couldn't wait to hear what she thought of my new product.

"Girl, that stuff ain't nothing but the truth," she said with a drawl and exaggerated emphasis. Her eyes were nearly closed when she was standing up in front of me, slightly bent over. And she scratched her back lazily. "Where you get that from, Kee?"

I told her I got it from my peeps and she asked me if I had more. I told her that I did and I now had it for sale. I was excited to begin this new gig, but I couldn't help but notice how stupid she looked, standing in front of me barely able to keep her eyes open. If you didn't know anything about a dope high, you'd just think she was sleepy. Why would anyone want something that made them look as dumb as she looked?

"Girl," she started again with that exaggerated, slurred voice. "I'm gonna tell everybody about this. This is some serious fire. I got ten dollars. I want a dime of that fire."

Still unaware of how heroin sold, I gave her another .2 grams as if I was selling her crack.

She thanked me and grabbed a dollar from her pocket. She folded the heroin in between the money and stuck it inside of her big ole FFF-sized breasts. Only after she stowed away the heroin did she tell me I was giving away too much dope for the money. In her slurred and barely coherent speech, she explained to me how the dope game went. It was different from selling coke, and she had enough sense in her to give me this friendly advice that I'd lose money giving away this much heroin.

I appreciated the little "Introduction to Heroin" spiel but got irritated by her zombie-like presence. No one could listen to that kind of speech for any more than five minutes. I just wanted her out of my house. I thanked her and half pushed her out the door.

Marcus was sitting in the living room this whole time and saw it all. He was as green to dope as I was. But he understood Martha's explanation of how to sell it better than I could, and he appreciated that heroin's worth was worlds apart from the price of cocaine. Seeing that he was catching on more quickly, I suggested he should bag it and show me what Martha was saying. It was confusing for me and I didn't want to deal with it. I already had enough going on selling the coke. I couldn't learn everything I needed to know about selling heroin in such a short time to launch our second hustle.

Martha came back a few hours later with more money. This time though, she wasn't going to get the lookout I gave her the first two times. The trial was over, and now it was real business. From there, word spread around faster than fire about my second hustle. From Martha my clientele grew exponentially, and my regulars and their people lined up to get my work, both coke and dope, like how people lined up at the stores when new Jordans were being released.

In the hood dope was referred to as "boy" or "train," and cocaine or crack was called "girl." Together, the girl and the boy brought me unbelievable amount of money. Too much for me to handle alone. I had to ask Marcus to handle the train while I continued with the girl. He stepped right in and did what I asked of him. Honestly, I don't know any hustlers that would've turned down the chance of making money without having to spend some to get it. But that was the way it was between us. He was my boo, my hustling partner, and my protection. In return I kept his pockets right because I couldn't have managed without him.

Things between us became more relaxed and more familiar. We shared everything like a true couple, and it made me feel that much closer to him. He began to drive my car whenever he needed to do things, even picking up Maurice and bringing him back to the house to chill. But Maurice, being a friend to Marcus for many more years than I'd known him, very soon noticed something different about Marcus.

"Hey Marcus," Maurice said. "Run me to the store real quick to get something to eat?"

It never takes too long for munchies to kick in for anybody who smokes. That was good; I needed to pick up something from there anyway. "I'll come along," I said, sitting up from the living room sofa where Maurice and I were watching television. Marcus was at the kitchen table bagging train.

"Alright," he said. "Give me a minute to finish this. You guys wait in the car for me."

We all got up and put on our shoes. Marcus was soon finished and he was putting the product away. "I'll just hit the bathroom and I'll be there."

Maurice and I both grabbed our coats and walked to the car. We waited in there, saying random things or sitting in silence. I was in the front passenger seat and Maurice was in the back. Almost ten minutes later, Maurice started getting impatient. Just as he started to complain, Marcus came out. When he got into the driver's seat, he kept rubbing his nose.

Maurice fired off. "Dawg, what the hell have you been doing? Got us just sitting here waiting on you!" He was upset, but it was no big deal to me. It wasn't like I was in a rush to get anywhere, and I didn't think Maurice had anything else to do either. I couldn't understand why he was so mad.

Marcus responded calmly, "I told y'all I had to use the bathroom. That's what I was doing." He rubbed his nose some more and wiped it on his sleeve.

Maurice calmed down in the back seat.

I asked Marcus, "What's wrong boo? Are you alright? Why do you keep rubbing your nose?"

"Oh I'm alright. When you cut up train the dust from it floats in the air, and some got in my nose. That's why I keep rubbing it. It feels like it's still there."

That made perfect sense to me, but Maurice grunted in the back as if he was irritated by Marcus's answer. I didn't understand what was happening, but I could feel the tension growing in the car. We drove off, but Maurice kept quiet the entire ride. Either something was going on that

I didn't know about, or Maurice was having a man period and blowing Marcus's ten-minute bathroom break out of proportion.

Before we got to the store, we stopped to grab something to eat, and after that Maurice wanted to go home, so we took him. Marcus was driving slower than normal. His voice had deepened and he never stopped sniffing and tugging at his nose. There was absolute silence between both guys, which was definitely abnormal. We pulled in front of Maurice's house, and Maurice jumped out the car, but not before grunting again in displeasure. He said nothing specifically to Marcus and walked off after a distant, chilled, "Talk to you guys later."

I didn't ask Marcus what was wrong with Maurice; I figured he only knew as much as I did. Only much later would I look back on this day and understand it all, and I wish Maurice had explained himself, if only to me.

Over the next couple of months, Marcus and I kept up the same routine, selling plenty of both drugs and seeing my re-up guy. Even with our growing client base and constant hustling, I maintained a clockwork routine to make sure my customers always had product from me and that I always had money coming in. But in the midst of this regularity, I began noticing a strange car sitting across the parking lot from my crib. It only was there on re-up days. I didn't recognize whose car it was. Neither did I ever see anyone getting in or out of it. It gave me an uneasy feeling, but since I couldn't figure out what it was, I didn't let it deter me from my hustling. By now, although I had gotten a hang of the ins and outs of selling train, I let Marcus handle that so I could manage the coke side of my gig.

* * *

ONE FRIDAY EVENING, Jay had already come by to get the boys for the weekend, and Mom was down the street over at Aunt Janice's house. Marcus and I were in the house alone. We were just chilling on the sofa when he turned to me and said he had a question for me. He seemed hesitant, and maybe a bit nervous.

"What is it, boo? You can tell me anything." I rubbed his shoulders to assure him. It was true. I trusted him.

"Boo, I want you to try something with me."

I was taken aback just a little. I truly trusted Marcus, but that was a little more open-ended than I was comfortable with. "Boo, you know I trust you. But I guess it depends on what it is."

He looked nervous again and tapped his fingers on his knee. He shook his head as if to shake out the idea of asking me the question.

I was a little alarmed. That kind of hesitation usually meant bad news. But it really could've been anything. I had no idea. So I encouraged him. "I'm sure it'll be ok," I said with a big smile. "Why won't you just come out and say it?" Maybe he wanted to propose, for all I knew, but whatever it was I wanted him to know he can be comfortable with me.

"Just tell me you'll say yes."

"What? What kind of sense does that make? I can't just say yes to anything. It could be something crazy! Did you get into a dare situation and tell your boys I'd dance for them?"

"No, no. it's not like that," he said, rubbing his hands together. "Do you trust me?"

"Of course, boo. You know I do. See, I trusted you enough to let you in here, be around my boys, and you handle my money, right? Of course I trust you."

"Well, just say yes you'll do it."

I paused and looked him in his eyes. He was serious. He had given me no reason not to trust him, so I gave in. "Okay. Yes, I'll do it."

He let out a brief sigh of relief.

"Well? What is it?" I was impatient to find out what he made me go through all that for.

He kissed my lips and asked me to have a seat at the kitchen table. Excited, I didn't delay. When he walked in the kitchen I was already at the table. But I was confused—he wasn't carrying with him a little jewelry box, a platter of cookies, a book, a car tire, or anything else in the world. Nothing would have confused me more than what I saw in his hands: my heroin shoe box. The smile on my face froze.

"What, why are you looking at me like that?" he asked as he sat down.

"Because you told me you wanted me to try something. Why do you have the shoebox in your hand?"

"Shhhh. That's because what I want you to try is in this box."

All smiles were gone, wiped completely from my face. "*What?* What do you mean?" I honestly did not understand.

"Just chill, boo. I got you. I asked you if you trusted me. Just chill."

With his calm demeanor and persuasive tone, I calmed down and watched him. He proceeded to open up the shoe box and take out a piece of dope wrapped in Reynolds wrap. We were told by a few dope heads that keeping train in Reynolds wrap preserved its freshness. We took the advice and ran with it. The box held individual packs of dope for sale, all weighed and wrapped, ready to go. Each piece of Reynolds wrap and its content sold for twenty dollars. Marcus opened the foil and removed the train. Pulling a dollar from his pocket, he put the egg inside of it. He folded the dollar bill in half with the dope inside, then he used a lighter to crush it up. He opened the dollar and used his pinky nail to scrape the train off the sides of the money. When he was done, there was a little pile of crushed dope inside. He dipped his pinky nail inside of the pile, putting a little on the inside of his nail. He looked at me and put it to my nose.

I wasn't sure what to do, so he gave me instructions step by step. First, I had to hold one nostril. Then, with the other nostril free, I bent down and sniffed the dope. I repeated it with the other nostril, exactly as he instructed. I was too confused, surprised, bewildered in the moment to think twice about what Marcus had just gotten me to do. I still didn't know what dope did to human bodies. But Marcus was my boo and I loved him. If he was doing it, that must have meant it was okay.

After I sniffed the dope, he took a couple sniffs himself. Then he folded the bill containing the rest and put it in his little fifth pocket. He put the box back in the room and returned with weed and a blunt. When he was done rolling up, he lit the blunt, hit it a few times and passed it to me. Before hitting the blunt, I hadn't really felt the dope, but I felt instantly sick after hitting the blunt a couple of times. I raced to the bathroom, feeling like I had to vomit. As much as I smoked weed I never had that problem.

Marcus followed me to the bathroom. Rubbing my back, he asked me if I was okay. "Was I okay?" What a stupid question. For one, I couldn't answer because I was busy vomiting my guts over the toilet. The first thing I did when I could catch a breath was ask him where this sudden sickness came from. Marcus explained that it was the dope that made me vomit like that, but he assured me that after I got used to the dope, it would be the best high ever.

He was right. Fifteen minutes later, I found myself feeling something I never felt before. I was past cloud nine. Now I understood why people were going so crazy over this stuff. I had a gold mine that I knew absolutely nothing about.

No more than an hour after my introduction to heroin, Biggs tapped on the door and came in with his girlfriend. Marcus and I were still high and sitting at the kitchen table. Marcus rolled another blunt for Biggs and his girl. I tried my best with everything in me to straighten up, but it felt as though I couldn't control my body. I must have looked like how Martha looked in front of me that day, as I fought to keep my eyes open. Then I had to vomit again, and leaning against the toilet, on the bathroom floor, I wondered if Biggs had noticed. After vomiting for the second time, I splashed cold water on my face hoping it'd refresh me and waken me a little. No, I felt even more high.

Biggs tapped on the bathroom door and asked if I was alright. I think he noticed. Trying still to pretend all was well, I opened the door and said I was just sick for a moment but was fine now. I joined them back at the table. I couldn't bring myself to look up at Biggs, but I could feel his eyes on me the whole time. Whether that was true, he never questioned me.

* * *

AFTER MY VIRGIN encounter with dope, my clockwork routine had a new element—sniffing dope. But I carried on with hustling and continued to bring in money. There was some kind of change in me that I was sure everyone had noticed. I used to be full of spunk and life, and now I was mellow, more settled down. The folks weren't feeling this new me, I could tell even though no one never said anything. Neither were they feeling Marcus any longer. I couldn't blame them though. He had come into my world and introduced me to something I never would've done. At the time, though, I didn't think much of it all and thought I was only having fun with it.

One day Maurice dropped by unannounced. It'd been weeks since we last saw him. He used to come every day, but after that one day when Marcus took a ten-minute bathroom break, he stopped coming around. When he showed up at the door, I was glad I wasn't high. But Marcus had already been sniffing. It didn't seem to affect him the way it affected me. A couple of sniffs along with a blunt lasted me through the day. He had a much higher tolerance.

Marcus and Maurice dapped each other up when Marcus let him in. All the time apart made them miss each other, and they picked things up right where they left them. They rolled up and smoked as usual while I cooked in the kitchen. I didn't bother hitting the blunt because I felt too sluggish and tired. I preferred my bed, though the money wouldn't allow me to go to sleep. And after cooking dinner I joined them in the living room, and Marcus decided then to get more cigarettes from the store.

Almost immediately after he left, Maurice started, as if he'd been waiting for this opportunity. He came right out and warned me of the dangers I was headed toward. He wasn't lecturing me, and I already kind of understood. At the same time, I didn't *really* understand. How could I? Life was the same as before. I was bringing in money. Marcus and I were close just like before. What harm had we done?

"What's going on with you and Marcus?"

"What do you mean?"

"Mane don't play stupid. You know damn well what I mean. Look, don't let this nigga come in your life and mess your life up. If you let him, that's what's going to happen. You got it going on. You don't need that clown. Don't let him be your downfall, and I'd better not find out your ass is sniffing dope."

I must have looked stupid at that time, if my face reflected even a bit of the confusion and hurt I felt inside. What he said pierced right through my heart. Maurice was right, but he came too late. It didn't change the fact that Marcus was still my boo, that I'd already done it, that

I'd continue doing what felt good. As long as I continued to get money, stayed fly, and take care of my kids, there was nothing to change.

I sniffed dope because I liked it, not because I needed it—so I thought. I didn't even notice that I had forgotten my goal of making and saving money, of getting to the top, becoming kingpin. I was getting high every day. Every now and then, I remembered what Maurice said. But the bond between Marcus and me was stronger than anything else, drowning Maurice's friendly warnings. What felt so good couldn't possibly be my downfall. And maybe Maurice was just jealous of what Marcus and I had with each other.

My use increased over time. I had gone from smoking weed to sniffing dope, to popping valiums and smoking cigarettes. Whatever my man turned to, he got me into. That was fine, though, because he still stood by my side. I felt protected, safe, and life was going to be ok.

Soon, the reality of my drug-using behavior began to dawn on me, if even slightly.

About two months after my first heroin use, I woke up violently early one morning from a dream. It felt so real. It felt as though I was there watching it all with my own eyes. I jumped up out of my bed in a sweat. Still shaken by the dream, I walked into the bathroom and looked at myself in the mirror. I ran the water, unsure of what I was about to do next. Brush my teeth? Drink the water? Wash my face? I couldn't think. So I turned off the water and sat down on the toilet.

Everything in the house was as quiet as a mouse. I was the only one awake and my dream troubled my mind. Was it trying to tell me something? Was God warning me? Should I take the dream as a warning? How could a dream be so realistic?

I went back to the bedroom and sat by the window after grabbing some weed. As I cracked and rolled a blunt, I twisted open the blinds to look out the window. Right across the parking lot was that same strange car sitting. I tried to recall if it was my re-up day. And it was.

"What's wrong boo? You alright?" Marcus was awakened by my movement and sat up in the bed.

I was startled by his voice because I didn't know he was awake. I smiled at him as I lit the blunt.

"You look like you got something on your mind," he said, rubbing his sleepy eyes."

"Yeah, I had a crazy dream and it woke me up out of my sleep."

"You want to talk about it?"

I turned around to peep at the car as I began telling him.

"I dreamed that there were a ton of police surrounding my house and they kicked down the door. They searched the house and found drugs and stuff. They put me in cuffs and took me downtown to the lockup. I mean, I actually saw myself walking to the police car handcuffed as if I was right there. It just seemed so real, I mean so real. I never had a more realistic dream in my life. Do you think that dream is trying to tell me something?"

"I don't know, boo. It might be."

At that moment, I suddenly noticed a pain shooting down my back. It felt like I had been in a car wreck or something. "Ouch!" I said, holding my back as I walked back to the bed.

"What's wrong, boo?" Marcus asked again. "You sure you're ok?"

"Yeah I think so. It just feels like I've been in a car wreck or something. My back hurts."

"Oh," he responded softly.

I was slightly hunched over because my back was in too much pain to stand up straight. He asked me to come to him. When I got in bed, he grabbed my arm and gently pulled me into his chest.

"Look, dope is an addictive drug. Your body needs it once you get hooked on it. After you become addicted to it, if you don't have it, you get sick."

"What do you mean *sick*? Like vomiting?"

He looked thoughtful, if a little somber. "It's like your body start going through different kinds of changes. There's different kinds of sickness. Some people experience body aches like what you feel right now. Some people have nose and eye runs. I mean different people have different symptoms, but that's what's wrong with you. Man, boo, I never meant for it to get this far. I feel so bad and that's so messed up on my part." He hung his head low. He looked sad, regretful.

I felt sorry for him. I knew Marcus loved me and that he never meant to hurt to me. I didn't think it was that big of a deal anyway. I could handle a bit of backache. "It's okay, boo. Just a bit of ache. It'll go away before we know it," I said, putting my palm to his cheek. "What's done is done, yeah? I'll be better soon." I lifted his head up and gave him a kiss. "I love you, boo."

With teary eyes, he said, "I love you too, baby."

It really did not feel like a big deal. My ignorance about heroin at that time meant I was still green. He still failed to explain it to me in its entirety. I thought for sure that at any time I could stop, just like I could stop smoking weed any time I wanted to, and the worst thing would only be feeling achy like after a car accident. Boy, was I wrong. Maybe I never really understood crack cocaine either. Maybe people smoked that stuff because they *needed* it, not just because they wanted it. Maybe that's why they sold their bodies in exchange for money to get it.

Whatever the case, I had a newly discovered desire, and soon I would become my own best customer. I didn't even have to go out in the streets and buy it. Marcus never told me that if I wanted to stop using, I could—just take a few days, endure the back pain, and I'd be ok without dope. I thought I had to continue using it, and I didn't mind it. There was no difference between dope and weed, except dope felt so much better. I'm sure if I knew that all I had to do was give it up for a few days and endure the back pain, I would've never touched it again. Had he went into depth detail with me about dope, I likely would've reconsidered my use. But he didn't so I kept using, thinking it not a big deal. There was nothing to worry about.

Marcus and I continued doing our hustle, but I began having occasional thoughts about not wanting Marcus in my life any more. I shouldn't have to take care of a fully grown man. My children were my only responsibility, and if an adult was going to take care of another adult, it should be a man taking care of a woman, not the other way around. I got that everyone had ups and downs, and I didn't mind helping Marcus through a rough patch. But it wasn't right for him to stay down.

I also began wondering if Marcus truly loved me. If he did, why would he have gotten me into something I didn't know how to get out of? Maybe he wanted to be with me because I had money. That couldn't be it, he didn't know at first. Maybe he somehow saw that I was the type that would provide for him. Maybe I'd just tell him that it wasn't working anymore.

* * *

I WAS DRIVING through an apartment complex on my way to a store one evening. I sat at a red light, heavy in thought, but I was brought back to reality by a car passing by on the other side. It had a Maryland license plate. And it was fancy. A fancy type of Mercedes Benz I had never seen in my life. The car alone looked like money. The windows were thick and looked bullet proof or something. Time seemed to have slowed down as the light turned green and that car and mine passed each other. I tried getting a look of the person behind the wheel of this fancy, but there was no way I could see under the evening sky and through the tinted window.

But whoever that was behind the wheel honked immediately, clearly impressed by what they saw though I couldn't see them. He rolled down his window and signaled for me to turn around. But I couldn't do just that. No one could order me around. If he wanted to speak with me, or the chance to do that, he needed to be a gentleman and approach me appropriately. To give him at least a slight chance, I stopped and pulled over the car. If he wasn't worth my time, though, he wouldn't get it. I needed to be home soon. Marcus had become insecure and been questioning my whereabouts.

My heart began skipping beats seeing through my rearview mirror that the Mercedes was approaching me. He must have impressed many women with this fancy car, which hinted at more wealth, a life of glitz and glamour. Everything you wanted would be within your reach. But nobody else's money meant extravagance for me. For me, what counted more is persistence, since I already had money of my own. Persistence meant he wanted me badly enough to show it and prove himself. I wasn't bought at a price. I was to be won with effort and a real heart. And I wanted a real man who had his act together. Whatever this guy was doing, he undoubtedly was successful at it. I had to put on my tough girl act to show him I wasn't an easy target, although truthfully, I was somewhat already attracted. His wealth meant he was successful, and no fool could pull that off. And now he was making an effort to meet me.

"Could I speak with you for a moment, Ms. Lady?" he said as his car pulled up next to mine. He smiled and I smiled back. Immediately he asked me if I could follow him into the parking lot.

I didn't object. How could I? He was respectful *and* respectable, asking so politely and flashing his pearly white teeth. His tone was gentle and reassuring. His dark, milk chocolate skin had always been my preference. His waves sat low on his head as if they were spun by the ocean's currents.

We both made a U-turn. I followed him closely and pulled my car right next to his. I got out of the car, laced in a snug black leather dress stopping just above my knees. I tugged at the dress to pull it down some, and I walked toward him, my hips swaying and my stride confident. My knee-length leather heels accentuated my garb perfectly. My diamonds sat around my neck and on my fingers, sparkling like the twinkles of the night sky. The twenty-inch hair brushed against my skin, framing my youthful, beautiful face. I too appeared to drip with money in my expensive attire.

He attentively watched in silence as I walked toward him. He was at a loss for words. He smiled, and the only thing he managed to get out of his lips when I came face to face with him was "Damn, you look even better than I thought."

I smiled. His compliment wasn't crass or flippant.

Extending his hand to shake mine, he introduced himself. "I go by the name of Cash, but my government is Rome," he said with a charming smile. "And you are—if I may ask?"

I was further impressed. He was really a gentleman, with a laid-back and very calm demeanor. Was he too good to be true? He was the kind of person I needed in my life, someone on the same level as me mentally, with the same zeal and outlook on life. "They call me Keisha or Kee, but Lakeisha is my government," I answered with a smile.

"You're fine, and with a sense of humor. I like that, I like that," he said. "So, what are you doing around these parts, Ms. Keisha, if I may ask?"

"I live not far from here and I was on my way to the plaza down the street."

Before I could get anything else out, he began speaking again. "Let me just be frankly honest. When I noticed you in your car there was no way I could let you get past me without speaking to you. I needed to stop you and find out who you are. Before we go any further, I just need to know if you have anyone special in your life, because I usually don't like to intrude. In this case though, I may have to reconsider."

I hesitated. It wasn't that I was going to be dishonest, because truthfully I was going to tell Marcus things weren't working out between us. He wasn't "special" to me anymore. At the same time, we were officially together, and I considered him my boo. Before letting my thoughts get the best of me, I answered honestly. "I'm not sure if he's that special. But there is someone fairly new in my life."

"How new?" Cash asked.

"In terms of relationship, we've been dating for about ten months, give or take."

"That's not long at all."

I think given the information, he felt he had a chance. A chance to take me from somebody that didn't mean much at all. Whatever he thought about my relationship status, whether it was significant enough not to disrupt or whether he should respect it, I didn't know and didn't offer more information.

"I'm not from here, as I'm sure you've probably noticed my tags. I live in Maryland, where I own several successful businesses. One of them is a motorcycle shop where my team and I make and sell helmets. We customize our customers' helmets. Let me show you something." He popped open his trunk using a remote and retrieved a helmet from his trunk. He brought it over to me. "This is the type of work we do," he said, showing me the helmet.

I was impressed yet again. The helmet was unlike anything I'd seen in Richmond.

"Look at the price tag," he said.

The white tag hanging from the helmet read $999.00.

"All of them aren't priced like this," Cash said. "Some more expensive.

Some less. It really all depends on the preference of the potential buyer. We also sell motorcycle equipment of all kinds."

Quietly, I listened. I liked his mindset. He was a man with a business mind, which was all the more appealing to me than his dark skin and pretty smile. He looked as though he belonged on the cover of *Jet* magazine, but too macho to pose only in briefs. I got lost in his words as I watched his gorgeous profile. There was absolutely no sign of the effeminate, which was another thing I liked. Maybe he could show me how to invest in something legal. I was all ears listening to him explain his business to me. He hadn't mentioned his other businesses, though he said he had several. I was almost certain I knew why he didn't talk about them.

"Look," he said, "you appear to be a loyal type. The fact that you've been with this guy for only a few months and you're unwilling to deviate is even more attractive to me."

Cash had already asked for my number and I was unwilling to give it to him. I told him Marcus lived with me and answered my phone whenever he wanted.

"What does he do, if you don't mind me asking?"

"You don't really want to know," I said, smiling and shaking my head at the same time. I gave him a look that suggested Marcus didn't really do much.

"Do you have children?" Cash asked.

I told him I had two boys and gave him their names and ages.

He said he had a son also. "Look, you can ditch this bum cat and never see him again. It doesn't sound like he's much worth holding on to. He should be in his own crib anyway, not living with you. I could have you, your children, and your things moved to Maryland with me, if you say yes. Better yet, if that makes you uncomfortable, I'm willing to get you your own crib until we get to know each other better. I know this may seem strange considering the fact we're perfect strangers. But I like you and I know you're easy to love. I can feel your spirit. You never know what the future holds," he said, giving me that killer smile. "I definitely believe in love at first sight." He smiled and grabbed my hand.

I could've melted as butter sitting in a cast iron pan on fire. Not only did he have it going on, but he was a mature gentleman. As fine as the best wine whose quality only gets better with aging. I was very tempted by his persuasive argument of why he'd make a better fit for me, but I just couldn't jump at the chance of relocating to another state. I took his number, however, and told him I would be in touch.

We hugged each other after an hour-long conversation, feeling like we weren't strangers. He wanted to kiss me, and I gave him my cheek. I kept his number and hid it where it couldn't be found by anyone. Maybe some time down the road, my situation would be different and I'd call him.

Back home, I thought about Cash, about his kindness and its contrast with Marcus, who got me into heroin for no reason. He never told me he had done it before, but looking back, it was clear to me that he was familiar with heroin and its effect. Cash stayed fresh in my mind in the following weeks and months, but I never called him. And I never got the opportunity to break things up with Marcus.

One day, Marcus proposed marriage to me, presenting me with a ring he bought with my money. Somehow, I was pleased that Marcus wanted something long-term with me, and that overrode everything I didn't like about him.

CHAPTER 10

LONG-AWAITED ENCOUNTER

Every other weekend was Jay's weekend with the boys. This weekend was his weekend, and I definitely needed the break. In fact, I needed a break from everything. And on Sunday, January 11, 1999, I got my break. Just not the kind of break I wanted.

That Sunday, I received a call from Jay telling me he was on the way to me with the boys. I was home alone. Marcus left just about an hour prior to visit his mother.

Almost thirty minutes later there was a knock. I knew for sure it was Jay, but I never opened my door without knowing who was on the other side first. "Who is it?" I said as I approached the door.

"It's Jay, Kee."

I opened the door and the boys hurried in, hugging me before I could close the door.

"I'll call your later," Jay said and waved me goodbye.

The boys wasted no time running into their room. They must have missed playing their gaming system while being with Jay. Then it occurred to me that Jay hadn't brought the bag of clothes that I handed him when he picked up the boys. But that was ok, when he saw it in his car he'd bring it back. Before I could finish the thought, there was a knock on the door.

"Bingo, there he goes with it!" I said to myself as I walked toward the door. "Who is it"? There was no answer. Standing at the door, I asked again, only this time I was louder. "Who is it"? This time there was an answer. But it wasn't the answer I expected to hear.

"It's the police, ma'am."

I must have heard wrong. I asked again. "Who is it"?

"It's police, ma'am," the male voice repeated.

I quickly looked out the peep hole. There were quite a few of those blue boys standing at the door. I quickly walked to the living room window and peeped out of the blinds. There was even more blue. I hurried back to the door because the male voice began to talk again. I was having a déjà vu. And it was just as my dream. Only it was real.

"Ma'am, open up. We know you're in there and if you don't open up we're prepared to come in."

I stood in front of the door, panicking, my hands trembling. I didn't know what to expect, but there was an abundance of drugs in the house. Drugs and a gun. Fortunately for me, the bulk of drugs was hidden. I could only pray they wouldn't be found.

"Ma'am!" the voice said again and I opened the door.

They were apparently narcotic officers, and one held a device that would assist in knocking my door in. I eyed them all. The officer standing in front began talking to me.

"There's been a report. Someone called crime stoppers and said that guns and drugs were being bought and sold from this home. And that the name of the person in charge of everything is Keisha and she has a blond hair weave." At that, the same officer held up a search warrant and said, "You must be Keisha because I see you've got the blond hair. We've got a search warrant to check your place."

They rushed in past me. My boys were still in the bedroom, having no idea what was going on. I sat quietly in the living room, trying to keep an eye on the police.

One officer standing near me began making sarcastic comments. "This surely is a nice place you have here. I wonder how you were able to afford all of this," he said looking around.

I didn't entertain him. Whatever he had to say was of no importance to me. I remained quiet, thinking about the bulk of weighed drugs I had hidden, and I watched the office dump my cereal onto the floor. They were in my refrigerator and freezer. I watch them go inside of the cabinets and miss the scale I knew they wanted. The police were everywhere.

After carefully examining my hall closets that turned up dry, they moved to the back of the apartment. I followed. I needed to watch them searching my place. I heard of how the police were famous for railroading people in all types of ways. They weren't about to get me like that. I wasn't going down behind something they planted because they couldn't find anything. When they got to my bedroom, I sat down on my bed and said a quiet and brief prayer. I knew I had been wrong but I found the nerve to ask God for something—not to let them go search the trash can. I used a thirty-three-gallon trash can in my room for dirty clothes and the bulk of my drugs. The plain eye couldn't see the drugs if one of the cops removed the lid; they would have had to really search through the clothes. They tore my room to pieces, not once thinking to go in the trash can.

"Thank you, Lord!" I mumbled somewhere under my breath. It must not have meant to be found. Boy, if they only knew that was where the gold mine was.

"Bingo!" one officer yelled as he went on top of my dresser and found heroin and crack cocaine.

"Got it!" another officer said, grabbing the firearm from my shelf.

They continued searching, adamant that there was more. I was nervous as heck when the plainclothes officer knelt down beside me. He said, "I know you're scared and you should be. We've been watching you for a while now, and it's really not you that we want. We know that you have a supplier, and that's the guy we want. I know you've never been in any trouble before. But if you help us we could help you. We'll be sure to make this thing disappear." He gave me his card and asked me to give him a call when I was ready to talk. If this guy thought I was going to be the snitch he suggested I was, he was dumber than his lying Pinocchio nose looked.

I mentally prepared myself at that moment for jail. I had long known knew that there were consequences to my actions though I never suffered them, consequences that only the best lawyers could get me out of. I was allowed to make a phone call since my boys and I were there alone. I called Jay and briefly explained what took place. Saying no more, he immediately turned right back around to pick up the boys. After Jay left the house with the boys, I was immediately handcuffed and read my rights. I was placed in a patrol car and taken to the city lockup. There, I was booked and fingerprinted. Afterward I was sent back to the cell until I was called to go before the magistrate. The entire process took all of three hours or more. I was tired and ready to go home.

My mind recalled the events of my life up to that time, but my thoughts lingered on the moment I met Marcus. I thought of how I started to decline steadily since inviting him into my home. I knew I had thought about that before, but I couldn't help it. I thought it again.

Finally, one of the deputy sheriffs came to the cell to get me. She walked me over to the magistrate's office, where they would determine whether I'd receive a bond. With no prior convictions and no reason to deny me bond, I was granted one. I was then allowed to make a free five-minute call to anyone of my choice. I called Marcus and tried to explain as much as I could in five minutes. I gave him the cost of my bond and told him to come get me. Just an hour later I was released to go home.

Back at home, I couldn't believe what I saw. My customers were all banging down my door; a great number of them showed up. I opened the door to what seemed like twenty of them at once. That night, I pulled an all-nighter as if I hadn't got arrested only hours before. You would've thought I learned my lesson, but I hadn't. I felt unstoppable, and the money was my motivation.

The next couple of months I continued with my life as usual, making money, sniffing dope, popping Valiums, and smoking weed. Time was approaching for me to make my first court appearance for an arraignment. I didn't know exactly what day it was, neither did I care enough to make sure. I was home that day when I got the dreaded phone call from my lawyer.

"What happened to you in court today, young lady?" she asked.

"Oh my Goodness! It was today? I thought it was tomorrow!"

"No ma'am, it was today. If you had called me and told me you couldn't make it, I would've been able to ask the judge to reset your arraignment. Now the judge has issued three felony capias warrants for your arrest. It will be in your best interest if you got yourself together and turned yourself in as soon as possible. The judge sought a mandatory thirty days per charge. You'd only have to do half the time per charge in jail."

I prepared to do my forty-five days. The night before I turned myself in, I gave Marcus a couple of rules. "Number one, do not let *any* females in my house while I am gone. It doesn't matter who they are. Except my mom. Number two, be very careful with your spending because I don't just blow through money. I'm a saver and that's how I got what I got." Despite my heroin habit, I was still on top of my A game. Maybe not the way I would've been prior to my introduction to heroin, but I was still there. Those two rules I told Marcus were the most important to me. Other than that, nothing else really mattered. Jay had already agreed to keep the boys while I did my time.

The following day, Marcus drove me to the hideous place where I'd turn myself in. We had a great conversation on the way there, and it eased my mind a little, though not nearly enough. He pulled up to the front of the building, but I dreaded getting out of the car. Marcus got out and walked over to my side. He opened the door for me and grabbed my hands. He helped me onto my feet and, pulling me toward him, hugged me tightly. We kissed and he grabbed my face, looking me into my eyes. He told me he loved me and that he was there for me. He also told me my time was going to go by fast and that there was nothing to worry about. He reassured me that he had everything under control. I believed him. He sounded so convincing.

He threw his arm over my shoulder and I wrapped my arm around his waist. Together we walked inside the jail building. It had been a long while since I visited Jay there, and it felt awful. I walked up to the window and gave my name to the young lady behind the glass. I told her I came to turn myself in to do forty-five days. She told me to have a seat and someone would be right with me.

We both took our seat, but I wasn't settled. I was a nervous wreck. I wanted so badly to walk back out of those doors and go home. Not quite ten minutes later, a brown uniformed deputy came over to us. On her hands she wore plastic gloves as if she were dealing with the diseased or something. She brought a clipboard that had pieces of paper she used to jot down my information. Moments later she asked me to stand up and place my hands behind my back. I did what she asked. I felt like crying, but I didn't. I was a big girl, and I was going to survive those forty-five days. I kissed Marcus goodbye and we went our separate ways.

The deputy walked me back to the female side of the jail, where I was asked to remove all my clothing. I was also asked to bend over, squat, and cough. It was humiliating and only a pervert would sign up to look at female coochie all day long. I wondered if they got a kick out of watching naked women. This was a part of the jail procedure everybody had to go through to make sure nothing illegal got inside. I was given an armband and an ugly bright orange jumper. I traded my nice shoes in for ugly shoes in the same bright orange color. I was given a half piece of dingy towel and a little bar of no-name soap. At least the toothbrush looked half normal, but the toothpaste was a far cry. They gave me a thin green mattress for the metal bunks where inmates slept. The dingy sheets and the wooly cover looked just like the towel. She explained to me while walking me to the tier that if I wanted a wash cloth, I had to order it from the canteen. She then walked me to a temporary tier, where I'd stay until morning.

It felt like the entire process took forever. The people seemed inefficient and slow, and I was glad when it was all over. I was happy also that everyone was in their beds and the majority were already asleep when I walked on the tier. I didn't want to have to engage anyone.

Early the next morning everyone got up for breakfast. I felt sluggish with a little back pain but it wasn't as bad as I expected. I was hungry because I hadn't eaten since early the day before.

It seemed like the entire tier, one by one, walked up to me asking my name. They were all telling me I was pretty and they loved my blond hair. I found it unusual for so many women to compliment another woman. Women were usually jealous or threatened when they saw a good-looking woman. Although they were friendly, almost all of them, young and old, looked like they were junkies. I wondered if that would be my fate too if I kept sniffing dope; maybe I'd end up looking like all of them a few years down the road. I couldn't think further. It was unthinkable.

I saw and watched the others in silence, until the heavy metal doors opened. The deputy yelled at the top of her lungs. "Come out if you're going to breakfast!" Everybody rushed through the doors, happy to be getting a meal. I guess I wasn't the only one hungry. The cafeteria clamored with loud conversations, but it all quieted down when I entered. All eyes were on me, the new member of this pitiable lot.

Then I heard someone shouted in my direction. "Hey Kee! What's up boo! What's up!"

I looked over and there was a light-skinned chick over to the side with her hands thrown up in the air. She had a big smile on her face as if she was happy to see me. It was one of my best money-making customers named Kitten. She was cool even though she was on drugs. Unlike with countless others, I was able to look past her use and see her for who she was. A cool chick that liked girls. She always told me how pretty she thought I was and hit on me every chance she got. It was always when I was alone in the crib when she came to get product. I only smiled at her boldness and liked her funny self.

After she yelled, the clamor resumed from all over the cafeteria, everyone shouting my name. I felt big. Like I was a don, a queen. A bright light in the midst of a gloomy and dark place. I tried looking in every direction in which my name was called. I began waving like I was Miss America.

I lined up for the food, and I scanned the typical jail fare on my plate—a clump of oatmeal, pale-yellow scrambled eggs, and shriveled-up sausage links. It looked far from appetizing, but anything was better than nothing. I sat down and dug into it. It was disgusting! The oatmeal was almost rubbery and utterly bland, the egg runny, and the sausages cold.

"I can't eat this. This is gross," I said, sliding the tray away from me, and my face couldn't hide the disgust I felt about this thing they called food. I thought I'd eat anything just five minutes ago, and now I'd rather starve before I ate that repulsive food. How could anyone feed humans such mess? I needed to go to the canteen if I were to eat anything in jail.

"You don't want that? I'll eat it," said the young lady sitting next to me.

"Be my guest." I slid her the tray.

Rather than eating, I was busy listening to the barrage of questions they shot at me all at once. I didn't care to answer, but I had nothing else to do anyway.

"Hey, where are you from?" asked one cute young girl sitting a couple of seats from me. She was there for some mess other than drugs.

I could tell she wasn't no junkie. I turned my head to look at her. "I'm from the Southside."

"Oh, what's your name?"

I told her my name was Keisha and she told me I was pretty. She wanted to know who did my hair. But before I could answer, a loud mouth sitting behind her started being rude.

"Hey shawty. Where did you say you're from again?" the manly-looking loud mouth yelled.

I was irritated. First, I was nobody's shawty. Even males approaching me in that way were unacceptable. Second, she was rude as hell. My face displayed my displeasure and I responded coldly. "Why?"

"What, what do you mean why? I was just asking, pretty girl with your blond hair and all that."

I had to block her out. Let her talk to my back. She didn't even have teeth in her mouth. She was the type they said would take your butt when you come to jail, a hardcore bull dagger that demanded what she wanted. She even looked like an old man. I could tell she was a junkie. It was bad enough I had to do forty-five days in a place with bad food, being away from home, my kids, and my money.

Back downstairs I was classified and placed on a different tier. Approaching the new tier with my blanket, mattress, and everything else dingy they gave me, I was greeted at the doors by a couple of women who were willing to help me carry my temporary belongs. One of the women grabbed a few things from my hands and escorted me to a free bunk that was near hers. Placing my mattress on her tight and snug made bed, she dressed my mattress, making it look just like hers. I was a clean young woman and I knew how to make a bed. But the way she made up that mattress had me second-guessing myself. She did it like she was a professional. Either she worked at some hotel that trained her, or that was just a jail thing everybody knew.

She introduced herself as Alana and asked me how long my time would be. She skipped asking my name. I'm guessing she already knew it. I told her I had to do forty-five days and why. That was the beginning of our jail friendship.

Alana helped me feel better about my transition from home into that awful place. She and I became close quickly as she schooled me on the ins and outs of the jail and how everything went. She also told me how most of the inmates were dope fiends, crackheads, and junkies. She was different. She kept getting in trouble for things like domestic violence and things of that sort. She had a year this time and was four months in.

My days there began to move fast. I was coping well and talking to Marcus every day. But just three weeks in, my conversation with Marcus took an unexpected turn.

It started off normal, just talking about what jail was like and how he was keeping busy out there. Out of the blue he confessed that he was horny and needed sex. My attitude immediately shifted. How could this nutcase of a bastard even come at me with such foolishness? He knew I was locked up and couldn't do anything to pleasure him. Did he want me to suggest that he go sex someone? What did he expect from me?

I was angry beyond words. I told him to go masturbate or something. I told him sex wasn't something that should've been up for a topic considering the circumstances.

"I didn't want to lie to you, boo. Just being honest." The way he said it seemed as though he wanted some credit for telling me the truth. It only made me angrier.

I was dumbfounded at the same time. I knew he was no good for me, but I didn't expect him to be so dense. What could I have done for him? I hung up the phone after reminding him I had only three weeks of jail time left.

Back at my bunk, I got lost in my thoughts of Marcus. Had I truly known him? Maybe even from the very beginning he wasn't who he appeared to be. I no longer had heroin in my system, being long past the back pains and jitters of not having dope. Now I was thinking clearly. This was a reality check for me, and I told myself that things were going to be different when I got home. I hadn't come up with a plan yet as to how, but I knew I was going to take back charge of my life.

That same night I had another dream, as realistic as the dream of the police coming for me. In the dream, my children and I were in Florida for a vacation. I lost my purse and we were there stranded without food, money, or a place to go. We were wandering about when I met an older lady. We began to have a conversation and I told her my children and I were there on a vacation but I'd lost my purse and didn't have money for food or to get home. She invited my children and me to her place to have dinner. While we were there, she loaned me the money to fly home to get funds to come back and get the children. I agreed. Both she and her husband took me to the airport and saw me off on my flight. I was anxious on the plane. I had no idea why. I could only stare at the half-naked young lady who watched me the entire flight. I had no idea who she was.

When I got back to Ruffin Rd, it was sunny outside, just like Florida. But I couldn't get into my own apartment since I had lost my keys. I knocked, but the door pushed right open and I walked in. The apartment was empty; no one was there. My bedroom was a straight shot down the hallway. I noticed the bedroom door cracked slightly open, and the bathroom door was shut. I heard faint music. "Hello!" I called out but no one answered. Reaching my bedroom door, I pushed it open. Sonja was sitting on my bed in a white t-shirt and nothing else. She saw me and jumped to her feet. She started dancing to the faint music that played in the background. When I started to question her, the bathroom door opened and I turned to see Marcus walking out of the bathroom wearing only boxer briefs and holding a wet wash cloth in his hands. He paused at the sight of me and looked shocked to see me.

In my dream I beat Sonja and dragged her down my hallway by her hair. I told her I'd kill her if I ever saw her again. That was the betrayal of my life. Thank goodness it was only a dream. Or was it? The sound of a loud voice awakened me early that morning.

"*Power on!*" the deputy shouted through the double doors onto the tier.

I was sleeping so deeply that I missed breakfast. Alana didn't wake me, but it was okay. I'm glad she didn't. I jumped up and headed for the nearest open phone. I called Marcus and anxiously waited for him to answer. I had to tell him about my dream. It felt realistic, and for all I knew, it *could* be real. Shortly before my arrest, Sonja had popped back into my life. We didn't see each other often, but we remained friends. Marcus knew she was my girl.

He never answered. The phone just rang. I called five times or more and still there was no answer. That was strange and definitely different. The entire time I had been in jail, Marcus made himself accessible to me through these phone calls.

With the nightmare fresh in my brain, I decided to call Allison, my nosey neighbor whom I secretly paid to watch my house while I was away. Marcus had no idea. She was my second set of eyes while I couldn't be there. She answered her phone immediately as if she was waiting for my call. After the phone was connected through the operator, before I even said anything, she wasted no time telling me how Sonja was just at my house the night before. She told me she was at her window when she saw Sonja pull up. She had come around two in the morning when everyone was supposed to be asleep. She was wearing a long trench coat and heels.

I listened intently to her details, thinking how it sounded like something from a movie. Allison said she sat by the window waiting to see Sonja come out of my house and leave. And it wasn't until six that morning when she left my house, still wearing her coat and heels. I was furious! I asked if Allison knew where Marcus was. She told me he had to be in the apartment because my vehicles were there. I asked her to knock on my apartment and tell that clown to answer the phone. I also told her I appreciated her information. We hung up on that note and she did just what I asked.

I knew it was all true. Just like what happened in the cop dream came true, this dream was no dream. God had shown me in my dream exactly what happened. Still, it was amazing that Allison confirmed it before I said anything. I called home, and Marcus picked up on the first ring.

I knew I had to be wise in how I approached this. if I angered him, he could leave and take everything from me since I left all my things in his hands. I calmly told him about the dream. He pretended to be so busy talking with Maurice and whoever else was in the background that he couldn't hear me well. I wondered if those men were there and saw Sonja come in.

"Marcus!" I had to call his name several times to get his attention because he was unconcerned the entire time.

"Yeah, yeah. I'm here. Look, that dream was crazy and nothing like that would ever happen."

I noticed his difference. Not one time did he call me boo or baby, the things he'd often call me because he loved me. Usually I burned up my phone line talking to Marcus. That day, I didn't feel the need. I was crushed, knowing I was betrayed by both him and my best friend. I could only deal with this when I got home. This was betrayal of Rule No. 1 I gave him. Apparently my rules went right out of the window and it didn't matter what I said.

I thought so much over the next few weeks about what I'd do with my life when I got out, and the weeks rushed past. Soon, I was due to be released.

CHAPTER 11

BETRAYAL

I WAS LYING ON MY BUNK WHEN I HEARD A DEPUTY YELLING ONE morning. "McQuinn, pack your belongings! You're going home." I jumped up. But first I had to make sure the deputy wasn't messing with me. I knew my release date, and it wasn't time yet. She assured me that she was instructed that I'd be released four days early. I had no idea why but I asked no further questions.

I quickly went into the bathroom to freshen up. I don't think my feet ever held that speed before. When I came from the bathroom, Alana had already packed my things. I gave her a hug and told her I was going to put some money on her books and leave my canteen for her.

After going through the discharging process that was as tedious as when I got in, I was released to my freedom. Marcus waited outside for me although I hadn't called him. He must've been notified about my early release date. I wasn't happy to see him, but I hugged him because he hugged me. I now had a different view of our relationship. He wasn't the loyal type he claimed to be. I was. We were different breeds cut from different cloth. The blood that ran through my veins didn't run through his. If he was loyal to anyone, it was to himself, not me. I finally saw him for who he was. I no longer trusted him.

For the moment, though, I needed to get myself straight and then deal with Sonja. I decided for now to give him a free pass like most women do when they find out their man has cheated. We take it out on the woman as if she made him do what he did, instead of realizing that two willing parties make choices together. Just like Jay. And now Marcus.

On our way home I asked him to stop by the hair store, where I purchased some great hair dye and a new hair style book. First thing smoking, instead of going to my stylist who'd make me wait, I called Charlene up. She was my backup for when I needed my wig smoked urgently. She was excited to hear from me since she didn't know when I'd be released. I offered to pay her extra if she could do my hair immediately. She didn't decline. I told her I'd drop off Marcus first and come meet her; that way she'd have time to get things ready. When I came to pick her up, we gave each other a big hug.

On our ride back to my place we talked about what I missed. It wasn't much of anything besides hood stuff popping off in Richmond. Hardly anything major. She was disappointed and annoyed to hear Marcus was still living with me. She was never really fond of Marcus and didn't care to be around him. That wasn't anything different from the rest of my people; they didn't care for him either, except for Sonja, obviously.

It was only a few minutes between our trip from Porter Street to my spot in Ruffin Rd. I hadn't called Jay and my boys yet to let them know I was home. I first needed to handle this situation with Marcus and Sonja. When we walked in, we didn't see Marcus and Rock. They were probably being high in my bedroom, where they needed to stay. At least until I got my hair done and kicked it with my girl.

As Charlene got her equipment set up, I noticed how I felt normal, like I was back to my old self. I didn't have a craving for heroin. I grabbed a towel and all the things Charlene needed to do my hair, including weed and a blunt. Charlene sat patiently at the kitchen table waiting on me. She looked as if something was on her mind. Before sitting down, I threw the weed and blunt on the table and told her to rollup. After pouring myself a cup of juice, I joined Charlene at the table and our conversation picked up where it was left off. We rolled the blunt and lit it, passing it between the two of us as Charlene started on my hair. We were still kicking it the way homegirls do. Then the house phone rang.

I answered. "Hello?" There was silence.

"Hello?" I said again.

That's when the female voice began. "Hey boo, I miss you. I didn't know you were home. When did you get home? Never mind that, it doesn't matter. I got some liquor and smoke. I'm trying to come through a little later so we can get wasted." It was Sonja.

For a moment I had forgotten about her. But here she was having the nerve to call my house, probably expecting Marcus to answer. He must have not warned her about my release. His stupid mistake. I didn't alarm her. Neither had I any conversation for the slut of a traitor that was my best friend. If she had any sense she would've picked up on that. But she didn't. I guess she figured she'd play it cool so I wouldn't get suspicious. And I played it cool too to mask my knowledge of her betrayal. Obviously she didn't know the girl she grew up with. I wasn't going to let her off the hook easily, and I was going to show her how wrong she was.

As soon as I hung up, Charlene said, "Hey, Kee. There's something I've gotta tell you."

"Yeah? Shoot."

"You gotta promise though you wouldn't say anything."

I could never understand why people make others promise things like that. I told Charlene I couldn't do that. "Just tell it straight, Charlene." Whatever she had to say couldn't have been anything worse than what I already had on my hands.

"You know I've been staying with Sonja at her baby daddy's house. That clown is at work most of the time and has no idea what type of girl he got. Well, one night I was walking to the bedroom I would sleep in whenever I stayed. Their bathroom is right next to my bedroom. When I walked past it, I had to backtrack 'cuz I saw her from the corner of my eye. She was fully dressed but she wasn't. She had on a white laced teddy and some heels. She was standing in the mirror messing with her hair, and she had a nude-color trench coat spread out on the toilet.

"When I noticed the coat and heels, I knew she was going somewhere. You know how we girls do when we together. I said to her, 'Oh, where you going, trick?' She looked at me and smiled. You know, she usually tells me everything.

"I stood at the door of the bathroom smoking my cigarette because she had my full attention. She said she had a date. I wanted to know with who and why she was acting like a silly giddy kid with a secret, and why it was a secret to begin with. So I asked her. She told me that it was a secret that she couldn't tell nobody. I just had to know, so I kept questioning her. She made me promise I'd tell nobody, and I agreed. I figured I wouldn't know the guy anyway. That's when she said her date was Marcus.

"Marcus, Marcus, I thought. I hadn't heard of this cat before. And Richmond ain't big as nothing and everybody knows everybody. Until it hit me. I put two and two together and understood why it was a secret. I covered my mouth and said to her that I knew she wasn't talking about your Marcus. The only Marcus I knew, period.

"When I said that, that whore nodded her head yes. I told her right then and there, that when you found out you were going to beat her down. She told me that wasn't going to happen because I wasn't going to tell you. That I promised her."

Charlene sat down next to me. "But you're my girl. I can't keep something like that from you. You do remember that she's my cousin through marriage, right?" She said that as if to imply that she and Sonja were not of the same blood.

I felt like murder, hearing her tell me all the details. I don't think a person could be any angrier than I was at that moment. I was angry to the tenth power. And since I couldn't beat him, I was going to punish Sonja. Charlene had no idea I already knew. Her information was only more confirmation. I got up immediately after Charlene finished telling me the news and told her I'd be right back. I needed to check on something else.

I walked down the hallway into my bedroom. Marcus and Rock were in there smoking when I walked in. I politely asked Marcus for my money and product. He handed me only one box when there were always two. Reaching into his pocket, he pulled out the same knot of money he pulled out at the hair store earlier. Even though the one box was enough to raise my suspicion, and the little knot of money was a far stretch from what I left him, I didn't say anything. Maybe, just maybe, the lack of money was because he had just re-upped the product. But if that were the case, it still should've been more than one box.

I walked back in the kitchen and sat at the table with Charlene. I put the money on the table and opened the box. My heart dropped. I got up before counting anything and walked back to my room. I asked Marcus, "Was that everything in the box?" He told me it was. I don't know how it was possible, but my anger was taken up a notch. I'm sure at that point horns were peeking from the sides of my head.

I walked back into the kitchen and sat down to count. First product, then money. I was way far beyond disappointed. I went from mad to hurt. Hurt because everything I'd built was snatched away from me at the hands of a low life. I couldn't believe it. How did he do it? What had he done in the forty-one days I was gone? How could he be so irresponsible and mismanaged the money, money that wasn't his? I sat at the table with my hands covering my face. The hurt turned into a furious rage. All of this new information was too overwhelming all at once.

My thoughts were interrupted by a phone call from Sonja. She told me her baby daddy was dropping her off at the store down the street on Jefferson Davis. She wanted to know if I could pick her up from there thirty minutes from the phone call. I told her I would. I was past ready to unleash all my anger on her.

Charlene tried picking up the conversation again after the phone call. She could tell something else troubled me besides Sonja. She asked me if everything was okay. I couldn't hold it in. I was glad she asked that question. I fired off unintentionally at her about the loss of my money and product, how that low life cat blazed through my money.

"Shhh! Girl, he could hear you."

Even if he did hear me, his being in the wrong kept him quiet. Charlene had no words for me. Not knowing how to console me, she could only shake her head at all that was going on.

The thirty minutes Sonja needed to make it to the store flew by fast. She called again to let me know she was ready at the store. When Charlene learned we were going to pick up Sonja, she wanted to go home. She didn't want to be in the house with Sonja and me at the same time, when things were slated to blow up. I understood and took her home, but I didn't let her off the car without calling her a few bad names. If she was my girl for real she would've stayed and told Sonja to her face what she had done.

I dropped her off and went back home before picking up Sonja. I don't know why I didn't just pick her up. Maybe it was because if I were alone it would've been a homicide. Whatever it was, I couldn't stand to be alone with that snake. Marcus and Rock both climbed in my van, not knowing where we were headed. I asked Marcus to drive and I sat on the passenger side. I only told them we were going to the store but I never said why. They didn't know I found out about Sonja and Marcus.

First thing Sonja did after getting in the car was asking what took me so long getting there. I wasn't in the mood to answer any questions, let alone hers. I ignored her question and we drove off, headed for my place. Nobody said anything on the way. Maybe even Rock knew about the betrayal. I wondered at that moment if it'd been more than once. How many times did she have the satisfaction of screwing my man? I sat quietly, watching them cut eyes at one another through the rear view mirror. If I were the devil, I could've easily dragged them both to hell. It was only a few minutes before we were back at my place, but the awkwardness in the car made it seem like hours. I remained quiet, not one time opening my mouth even after we walked in the house.

Sonja and I sat at the kitchen table while Rock and Marcus headed for my bedroom. She began pulling all her "get wasted items" onto the table. She had valiums, heroin, weed and liquor. My anger subsided somewhat watching her crush up the dope. It was funny how she had the exact same concoction Marcus liked. Minus the liquor. That was something extra. But then again, who knows, maybe it was their thing. After all, the guy I thought I knew turned out to be a stranger. Before she had taken a sniff of her own heroin, she passed the twenty-dollar bill to me. What the hell, I felt like I needed to drown out everything. After I got my share, she passed me two volumes but I gave one back. The one on top of the dope with the weed was enough. I wanted to decline the liquor because that never was really my thing. But then again, neither were dope and pills. So what the hell, I grabbed a little glass.

After smoking half the blunt she and I walked to my room to join Marcus and Rock. Marcus lay on the bed while Rock sat on the floor. The conversation they were having halted immediately when we walked in. She gave the twenty first to Rock, and he passed it to Marcus. She joined Rock on the floor and handed out the pills and passed the blunt.

In a matter of minutes, the entire room was quiet. We all were in a befuddled, sozzled state, looking like four dumb zombies from the *Walking Dead*. I opened up my eyes when I heard her voice.

"Kee, take me to the store for some cigarettes?" She was standing up, but bent over to tie her shoe. That reignited my fury like nothing else. Within a second I was full of wrath all over again.

"Hell, no." I looked away. The chill in my voice got both Rock and Marcus to open their eyes. To all of them, my response came out of the left field.

"What's wrong, girl?" Sonja asked.

Since she asked, I let her have it. "Somebody told me that you and Marcus were screwing. You know what, bump all of that; Charlene told me you and Marcus were screwing." I could see the fear spreading over her face. I felt like I wanted to tackle her through my bedroom window, and she looked like she knew she had it coming.

She was now standing erect and denying the truth. "Charlene was lying. I have no idea what you're saying."

She had no idea of the other proof I had.

"Let's drive to Charlene's now and get things straight." She had the nerve of suggesting that. "Or I'll call my ride and they'll go pick up Charlene."

She could do whatever she wanted. I didn't care. So she called her ride to come get her, and they headed to Charlene's. I left my bedroom, leaving Marcus and Rock alone. I didn't feel like dealing with either of them. I only wanted to get to the bottom of the truth. For now, though, Marcus was off the hook and Sonja was my focus.

It took nearly an hour for the ride to deliver them both back. When I let them in, I was no less angry than an hour before. I took my seat back at the kitchen table, where I was alone, waiting for them. Charlene joined me. Sonja didn't bother sitting. She stood in the middle of the floor facing Charlene and me. I began the questioning.

"Charlene, did you not tell me that Sonja was creeping with Marcus and that she came to my house wearing lingerie?"

Charlene held her head down. Then she got a surge of boldness from somewhere and stood to her feet. Pointing to her own chest she began to speak. "Yeah, I said it. And trick, don't lie. You know you did it." She pointed her finger at Sonja.

Sonja shot back, all defensive. "What? That's a lie. I don't want no Marcus. That clown is broke. What am I gonna do with him?"

He was everybody's clown that day. I called him that quite a few times myself. But hearing her say that added insult to injury. She continued her loud argument while approaching me slowly and pointing to her chest. By now I was standing on my feet at a distance from her. I listened to her rant on. I was never the arguing type and had no more words for her. At this point, there was nothing more to talk about. She was guilty, they both were. But being the smarty pants she was, she continued to walk up on me while running her mouth.

"I can have any dude I want. Why would I want him? A broke useless bum that can't do nothing for me. He isn't good for nothing but looking good and sex."

Wait a minute. She just admitted that he was good for sex. She was bragging in my face that his sex was good. She was bold. But not bolder than my fist that punched her nose and lips at the same time. Like a rude, disrespectful child, she deserved to have someone beat some sense into her. After that, I don't remember what happened. I blacked out. I came to with her yelling, "Somebody get her off me! Get her off me!" I hadn't noticed Rock and Marcus standing there until Rock pulled me off her.

I punished her with everything I felt in me. I told that whore to get out my house and that I'd kill her if she ever showed face around Ruffin Rd again. She grabbed her purse and hurried out the door. I followed her outside just like in my dream. Rock followed me. I was done with her though. I only watched her stumble down the sidewalk and climb into the car with her baby daddy. I walked back in the house into some type of praise. They were telling me how I beat the life out of her. I had no idea what happened after I blacked out.

That night, Marcus got off with the part he played in everything. We spent the remainder of the night high and free.

Over the next year or so my lawyer constantly put my case off, buying me time because I wasn't ready for jail. Things hadn't gotten any better as far as my life was concerned. After getting out of jail, I returned to dope, and I couldn't bounce back with that habit going on. Having Marcus around didn't help. He had the audacity of becoming controlling even after his betrayal, and he drained what little money I managed to hold on to. Like the weak, young idiot I had become for him, I handed over everything I got my hands on.

The more I allowed him control, the more he took advantage of me. When his dope habit skyrocketed, mine did too since he was the one in control of the spending. For some time, I felt like his victim and could only accept whatever he handed me. In my rebellion, I started doing things he disliked. He didn't want me wearing pants or shorts that hugged my full hips and butt. That was everything in my closet, and there was absolutely no way I was going to replace my entire wardrobe. I didn't change that for him, and he became even more insecure as he got deeper into his addiction. He became paranoid more than ever before, anxious that I'd get someone else's attention who would take me away from him.

To get away from the suffocating environment at home, I'd go to Charlene's, where I felt comfortable venting to a friend. But one day, when I was about to head out to Charlene's, Marcus insisted that I stay. He threatened that if I went ahead, he'd make me pay when I got back home. I was not swayed. His bad boy image might have scared others, but I knew he wasn't all he was cracked up to be. I left and stay gone only a couple of hours. I brought Charlene back home with me only to have an excuse to leave again. I went to my bedroom after getting home, and he was lying across the bed. He asked me where I'd been. I looked at him in disgust, rolling my eyes without parting my lips. He stood up and snatched my car keys from my hand. He told me he'd be back. I knew he really didn't need to go anywhere because if he did he would've taken the van. He was in no condition to drive. Marcus was high out of his mind. I offered to take him, but he insisted to go it alone. I wrestled with him for a moment trying to get the car keys back, but I couldn't. He left, and I began to pray quietly.

No more than ten minutes later, I got a phone call that I wasn't ready for. It was Marcus's mother. She told me he was in a car wreck on Jefferson Davis and that I needed to go there quickly. My heart began pounding in my chest. It was just what I'd feared. I asked Charlene to go with me. I decided that it was best to walk since it wasn't far at all.

My mind was on my car the entire time we walked. It was far more important to me than Marcus was. I really didn't give a thought about him or his condition. I was terribly upset when I reached the top of Jefferson Davis and saw from a distance what had happened to my car. It sat in the middle of the intersection, crushed beyond repair. I knew immediately it was a total loss. Marcus wasn't there. They had rushed him to the hospital. I approached the car and noticed blood everywhere. I began retrieving my mail and things of importance to me from the car. I wanted to cry, knowing it was the last time I'd see my baby. Police hovered around the car, collecting whatever evidence they needed. I didn't understand why they treated the accident like it was a crime scene.

After gathering all of my things, I started walking away from the car, then I was stopped in my tracks when someone called out my name.

"Miss McQuinn! Excuse me, Miss McQuinn."

I turned to see the same detective that kneeled next to me by my bed and gave me his card a year earlier.

"You can't go anywhere, miss. You are under arrest," he said.

I was shocked. He retrieved the indictment from his suit jacket and opened it up so I could have a look at it. Pulling out his handcuffs, he started reading me my rights. Before he could cuff me I took my jewelry off and handed it all to Charlene. I whispered to her where I had drugs and money stashed in the house. While he was cuffing me, I told her go to my place and stay there and that I needed her by the phone in case I got a bond.

The police wagon soon pulled up and I was escorted to the downtown lockup. I was booked and processed for the second time all over again. Why? I hated going through that. Those deputies were so slow with their processing. I was taken before the magistrate and denied bond because of the previous capias I had. She told me I had to go before the judge to get a bond, and that I couldn't see the judge until the following business day. That meant I had to stay the night in jail. I didn't know whether I'd be given a bond. So much damage had been done to my life because of this guy.

I sat in the bullpen, waiting to get my free call. Within a few minutes the deputy came to the door telling me I could make my call. I hurried to the phone to put Charlene up on the news. I was still on the phone when I heard the deputy shout, "Hit the doors! An arrest is coming in." My eyes zoomed in on the officer and the arrestee with him. I couldn't believe my eyes—next to the officer was a very bruised, swollen, and limp Marcus.

I ended my conversation with Charlene right away, and with the agility of a leopard I sprinted over to them. I hugged my man, feeling bad for the way he looked. Neither had the officer or deputies objected. I kissed his swollen and stitched lips. I hadn't given him two thoughts since he wrecked my car, but seeing him like that was hurtful. His face was extremely swollen. They had taken him from the hospital too because of his warrant. I was unsure of what he was arrested for, but at that point it didn't matter. We were allowed to exchange a few words before being separated. I was then escorted back to the bullpen. Wasting no time, they began fingerprinting and processing him, and they did so faster than with me, perhaps because of his condition.

They were soon putting us both in the paddy wagon to be escorted to the jail. That was where I learned what happened to Marcus. Only a thin wire gate separated us in the wagon. I was able to look him in the face when he gave me the story. He told me he was driving down Jefferson Davis when he nodded off behind the wheel. He said a dump truck hit the car from behind and he did a three-sixty onto oncoming traffic. "After oncoming traffic hit me," he said, "I couldn't remember anything that happened afterwards."

He asked why was I arrested. I told him at the scene of the accident the police had an indictment for me. It was the same officer who wanted me to snitch that gave me the indictment and read me my rights. I told him his mom was the one who called and told me what happened. Before we could say more to each other, we were at the city jail. Three days later we both were given a bond, and his aunt got us both out at the same time. When we were released, I learned Marcus's real age; he was two years younger than me, not older, as he had claimed to be. Damn. It was always one thing after another with him.

Charlene was still at my crib when we got home, along with her son. She held it down like I asked her to and I was thankful to her for that.

After this second arrest, I was not like how I used to be. Before these arrests, it was an enjoyable and fun time selling plenty of drugs, getting plenty of money, and living the high life. But it had turned into a life of loss after loss and it was a struggle to maintain a dope habit. I sold drugs still, but nowhere near how much I was selling a year ago. From there things went down a spiral quickly. The more I got high, the less I cared about the things that once mattered to me. I no longer spent money to have my hair done, get my manicure, keep up my wardrobe. The hustler's ambition was no longer in me. I had been broken. I felt like there was no way of getting my life back. Still, even on my downward spiral, I clung on to the root of my downfall, Marcus.

My lawyer finally called me to discuss what she and the Commonwealth agreed upon if I accepted. She was aware of the indictment and said she had the indictment run concurrent with my other charges. I wanted to ask why she didn't come to my aid if she knew I was in jail. I shouldn't have had to waste three days in jail if my paid lawyer could've convinced the judge otherwise. I let the thought go, and we both agreed on a date to meet.

Seven days later, I was in my lawyer's office. We discussed the initial charges, which were heroin, cocaine, and a firearm. Because it was my first offense, the Commonwealth was willing to drop the heroin and gun charge if I agreed to plead guilty to the cocaine. She said if I accepted the plea my sentence would be ten years, with nine years and nine months suspended. I would only do three months of jail time. But, she said, if I wanted to fight, I also had the option of declining the plea offer and she would be right alongside me. In that case, my charge would go in front of a grand jury, who would decide my fate. The judge would no longer be a deciding factor in the case. My lawyer assured me that she was confident she would be able to get me the best outcome, whichever I route I chose, and that the decision was mine. She left the room to give me a few moments to think.

I pondered in silence, thinking over everything. I thought of my children. I thought of Marcus and the screw-up he had been to me. I thought of everything I had done and what I'd lost up till that point. I thought of what would happen to my place when I went to jail. I thought of Sonja. Then my mind turned to the thought of pleading guilty and what I would face if I went before a jury. I made up my mind that pleading guilty was the best thing for me, not realizing I'd soon be making the biggest mistake of my life—a plea bargain can never be expunged and would remain an indelible stain on my record that made everything on the other side of jail walls all the more difficult. I told the lawyer when she returned to the conference room that I couldn't take the gamble of going before a jury. I'd take the plea bargain.

On the morning of September 7, 2000, I went to court, confident of my decision. I stood while my charges were read aloud. My lawyer began the proceedings on my behalf. She told the judge that she and I were offered a plea agreement by the district attorney, and we agreed to the terms of the plea. Turning to the attorney for the Commonwealth, the judge asked for confirmation of the agreement. The DA acknowledged it and the judge accepted the terms of the agreement.

Turning back to me, the judge asked if I fully understood the terms I had agreed to. I answered in the affirmative. He asked me a series of questions, and I answered each honestly and respectfully. I gave him my full name, replied that I could read and write, and confirmed that I was not forced into the agreement. After these questions, the judge read me a brief statement. He then read my sentence of ten years, with nine years and nine months suspended. My lawyer requested that the judge give me time to arrange my caretakers for my children before turning myself in for the jail sentence. The judge granted me a week.

Those seven days went by quickly, and the morning of September 15, 2000, I turned myself in. How I hated that tedious process. The environment was still unpleasant, and the officers were still slow as molasses. As I waited, I thought about my dope habit and hoped I would survive in jail without it. I thought about the torture that awaited me. Three months of jail sentence. It hurt thinking about how I ended up here and how Marcus betrayed my trust. Sure, the betrayal involving Sonja cut me deep, but that wasn't the only way in which he betrayed me. He knew I trusted him and loved him. He knew that even though I sold heroin, I had not allowed it into my system before he convinced me to try it. That betrayal was what hurt the most.

After I was taken to my tier and got situated, I noticed that I felt more comfortable this time. It wasn't the strange place that it seemed the first time round. I felt now like I fit in with those already here. Those same no-name junkies now felt like my friends. I could bond with them now because I understood what I couldn't the first time. Some of the girls were in there all the time. It looked like there was no future for them. Maybe the drug had sucked the life out of them the same way it was doing me. I saw that if I didn't get myself straight, I'd be spending the rest of my life in and out of jail like they were. I was staring in the face of my future if I didn't change my life.

On top of my three-month jail stint, Marcus told me when we spoke on the phone that a thirty-day eviction notice was slapped on my door. Nothing came as surprising news to me. I had become used to the chain of downward spiraling events one right after the other. How could it stop as long as the devil was around me? I needed to get away from Marcus if I wanted to have any hope of regrouping my life. But it seemed like I was under a spell. I felt more sorry for him than angry. And if I did feel angry, I quickly forgot to be when I was around him. But now was a God-sent opportunity for me to figure out a game plan. I had two and half months to figure out where I'd live when I got out. My boys were again with Jay while I did my time. At least they had somewhere to stay even if I didn't.

As I made plans to emerge from my mess, Marcus made all kinds of promises to me over and over when we talked on the phone. He promised he'd have a place for us when I got home. I knew better than that. The truth was he was incapable of doing anything to better us. He was incapable of handling manly responsibilities. He proved that to me more times than I cared to remember. He also said he'd put my things in storage and keep my van safe. During the phone calls I knew he was high, and I couldn't wait to hang up.

Sitting in my bunk bed, I thought about how I was truly alone. My mind played back the scenes of my life that had been flipped upside down over the last two years. Before I invited the devil to come inside my home and ruin my life, I was one of the most loving mothers who provided her children with absolutely everything. I was a young, ambitious go-getter. I took care of those I loved. I became an independent young woman despite my upbringing. I was goal-oriented, although I didn't always have the right goals. How stupid of me to throw it all away for a cute bum! After he put heroin to my nose, he proceeded to sleep with my friend while I was in jail, even after I told him not to let women in my house. Now, I had lost my place, my children, and everything that I stood for.

The next day, Marcus told me he had already gotten a large storage unit and was boxing all my things up. I was a bit surprised to hear he was actually taking care of things. He tried his best to reassure me that he would have a place by the time I come home. I listened. Not only did I listen, but I think I almost believed him. He apologized for everything that had happened and said he was responsible for how my life crumbled. That admission helped more than I thought it would. Call me insane, but that five-minute phone call in which he admitted his wrongs and told me he was getting his act together had me reconsider everything. I decided against my intuition to give him the benefit of the doubt. I thought that perhaps he just needed to see that I saw him as a man, and he would make up for everything that happened. I believed things were turning upwards.

I spent my incarcerated days in quietness, having accepted it as my lot. I also was looking forward to a new life when I got out. I thought about the beautiful picture Marcus painted for me, and I fell in love all over again. He left the apartment and moved all my belongings into a storage. He was now in search of our new place just as he told me he was. I looked forward to seeing him come through for us, for both me and himself. After moving out of my place, he was homeless, so I hoped that for his sake he'd find a place soon.

I befriended a young lady, Tina, while I was in jail the second time. Thanks to her and the medication she gave me, I was able to ween myself from my habit. I slept mostly. That's what the pills were designed to make you do. At least that's how I felt. I took it only at night when I tossed and turned and couldn't sleep. I don't know what I would've done without her. She was also a heroin addict and understood my struggles. She and I became close during my incarceration.

I was glad to have Tina for support, because I needed it. Just weeks before my release, Marcus told me my storage was up for auction. Instead of taking two steps forward, which he deceived me into believing he would, he walked backwards. When he told me on the phone I'd lose everything I owned, I was hurt, confused, and my heart was crushed into a million bits. My photos frames that held memories of my children, birthdays, family. My clothing, my shoes. Everything. I wanted to know why, although it didn't matter, and he mustered the courage to tell me the truth after giving me excuses.

He told me he had to choose the largest storage they had, which cost the most, but after the first payment he didn't have any more money to keep up with the payments. He said he tried to buy as much time as he could, to borrow the money, but it just didn't work out. I cried. I think I must've drained every bit of water from my body. The only thing to look forward to now when I left jail was my van. There would be nothing else to go to.

Marcus promised on the phone that he'd get me all my things back. How could he expect me to believe that if he couldn't manage a storage fee of $200 per month? Did he think I was that dumb? Perhaps I was. I did believe every lie that left his lips. They say that people do things they know they could get away with. Maybe that's why Marcus did them.

Maybe that was why tragedy after tragedy kept occurring. Either that, or he was cursed. Somebody that would bring bad luck to anybody that dealt with him. I left him everything I had to my name, including close to a thousand dollars in cash. He told me he would flip the money and do what he needed to do for us. Apparently, he sniffed that money up, completely dropping the hustle. He kept apologizing and telling me how bad he felt. He said he was nothing more than a screw-up, and I agreed with him. At least he knew what he was.

Despite everything that continued to fail around me, Tina made me feel better. She and I were due to be released only weeks within each other. My time before hers.

On the morning of December 13, 2000, I was called to pack my things. I was being released from the jail. I was happy. Not because I was going home to a pleasant situation, but because I missed my children and badly needed to see them. I needed to hear their voices. To touch them. To tell them that everything was going to be okay just as before. I rehearsed every day during those three months how I would make it all up to them, and how I would never make them feel insecure or scared. I would become the mother I was before, and I'd promise them that Marcus would be out of the picture for good. I would prove to my boys that they were my priority, and I wouldn't sacrifice them for that bum Marcus. My boys would be able to count on me, who would be a soldier and fight to get our life back.

I walked out of jail, putting one foot in front of the other through the snow. I was positive about the future that my children and I could look forward to. I was positive that I'd get back on top despite these setbacks.

CHAPTER 12

A NEW LOW

Little did I know, Marcus had a different plan, one that didn't include my children. I walked toward the car. Waiting for me outside the jail was Marcus who greeted me. He hugged and kissed me. But I wasn't in the kissing mood. I was looking forward to a new life that he wasn't going to be a part of. I was starting over. I was drug-free now, thank goodness.

I didn't realize the car wasn't my van until I opened its door to get inside.

"Where the heck was my van?" I asked as soon as we drove off.

"Boo, I'll tell you as soon as we get home. Just not right now."

My heart did a dip in my chest when he said that. More bad news was coming my way.

"Well, can I go see my boys?"

Even that he wouldn't grant me. "My ride has to go somewhere so we can't do that. But we'll catch another ride later. I promise."

"Why the heck do we have to go in other people's cars? Where's my damn van?" I knew he said he'd tell me later, but I was entitled to know what happened to my property, the van I entrusted to him.

Calmly, he kissed my lips and repeated that he'd tell me when we got home.

I had no idea where home was, but I shut up and rode along. About twenty minutes later we pulled up at his aunt's apartment. It was a beautiful set of apartments on the south side of town, off Midlothian.

"What are we doing here? Isn't this your aunt's?"

"I'll tell you in a second," he said, extending his hand to help me out of the car.

His aunt was standing at the door to greet us. She hugged me and welcome me home. She was such as pleasant face to see, and her place was as pretty as she was. She had two younger daughters, who lived with her, and she had it going on. That was the same aunt who bonded both Marcus and me out of jail. By now I figured she was opening her home for us to stay. I appreciated her for that. She didn't have to; I was only Marcus' girlfriend.

Marcus and I sat down on the living room sofa, and he began explaining to me what happened to the van. He first felt the need to apologize again about everything. That alarmed me. I already knew that was an introduction to some bad news. I learned that apologizing before breaking the news was his way of getting me to accept whatever followed. He thought it'd soften the blow, but I was no idiot.

He was in Blackwell buying heroin, but as soon as he got it and drove away in my van, he was followed by the police. The cops might have had a warrant for his arrest, but he didn't know because all he could think about was the heroin in his pocket. So, he jumped out of the van and ran. He reminded me he had put the van in his mom's name before she went into the rehab program. And now, after he ran, the van was towed, and only his mom, who the van was registered under, could get the van back. But his mom was in rehab and wouldn't get out for another thirty days. By the time his mother was out of rehab and available to claim the van, so much fee had accrued that he couldn't afford it.

I had no words. That killed every plan I had. I thought I was going to at least have a vehicle to use for going to visit my boys and find jobs. I wasn't sure any longer how I should maneuver from there. The one thing I thought would help me get back on my feet was taken from me too. The only thing I had were the few items of clothing he kept from the storage.

He continued blabbering on, apologizing and assuring me how it would all be ok, then a horn blew outside and interrupted him. He walked over to the window to see who it was. As soon as he saw, he grabbed his coat, kissed my cheek and told me he'd be right back.

I was left alone in the living room. I looked at the Christmas decorations his aunt already put up, including a Christmas tree all decked out. I thought of my boys. I felt as though I had abandoned them. Marcus never mentioned them even once, making me realize they were of no importance to him.

What was I to do? Where was I to start? I had no money. No clothing. No car. Nothing. The only thing I knew was the streets. I never had anyone else to show me anything different. I was twenty-two years old and a high school dropout with two children. I had no work skills because I never held a job. I tried, but they never lasted longer than a couple of days. It was a waste of time to me. I missed out on too much money being away from home trying to work for pennies on a dollar. That made no sense to a young hustler whose ambition was money-driven.

I cried. I sat and thought and I cried even more. I felt as though my back were up against a wall with nowhere to turn. We couldn't stay with his aunt forever. I didn't want to. I was used to taking care of myself, providing for my own needs, since the age of fifteen. I had taken great care of my children. I had done so well, and then *this*. I was drowning in a sea too deep for me to swim in and there was no life coach to help me, and there was nobody to throw me a life jacket.

My thoughts were interrupted by the sound of Marcus opening and closing the door. He saw my distress and again promised everything was going to be okay. He wrapped his arms around me. Despite the trouble he'd gotten me into, his hug felt comforting.

"Boo, I've got a surprise for you. I promise it'll make you feel better."

I didn't know what to expect, but the thought of a gift lifted me. He got me something for Christmas, and that in itself was something to be happy about.

He grabbed my hand and led me down the hallway, stopping at the first room we reached. He told me that was our new bedroom, and he proceeded to give me a tour of his aunt's lovely place. We stopped at her bedroom. She sat on her bed, taking inventory of the lingerie she had for sale. She smiled when she noticed us there and continued what she was doing. Still holding my hand, Marcus led me into the bathroom and closed the door behind us. Now that we had privacy, I immediately tried to figure out where the surprise gift was. Marcus remained quiet the entire time. I pulled the curtain back checking the tub. It wasn't there. I checked the cabinets under the sink. It wasn't there either. Was it in the bedroom? I went to check and nothing was there either. I came back to the bathroom where Marcus was, and I was greeted by a mysterious smile on his face. In his hand was a folded dollar bill.

"Where's the gift?"

"What gift?"

"I thought you said you had something for me that'll make me feel better."

"Yeah, I do. This is what I was talking about." He opened the folded dollar bill, showing me the dope inside.

My face dropped.

"Oh, you thought I meant a gift when I said I had something for you. That's why you were in here looking around."

"Yes, that's exactly what I thought."

"Awe, baby I'm sorry. I didn't mean to upset you. But this will make you feel better though."

I had no words. Marcus had a way of driving away all my joy in an instant. He had a way of plunging me deep into a hole at the turn of a corner. To think he'd save money to buy me a gift was absurd. I felt stupid.

Turning back to face me, he took his long pinky nail and dipped it into the little pile of dope. Scooping just enough, he held his finger to my nostril and told me to sniff. It was déjà vu and, just like the first time, I didn't think twice. I had nothing to lose. We sniffed again, and again.

I noticed the amount of dope inside the twenty-dollar bill. I understood why he couldn't keep money. Every dime of what he did make was spent on dope.

My first day home and all of my plans were out the window. And I sniffed my troubles away. In the days that followed, he was always high, and he did ridiculous things while high, like singing silly songs that belied his guilt. One of the refrains he often sang was the one by the singer Ginuwine from his song "It wasn't me," and the words could not be more appropriate for the man who betrayed me. But why would anyone guilty of cheating sing something like that? Was he just dense, or was he that arrogant that he'd brag about it to my face?

One day, the truth would come out of him, and this was the day. We were alone in a hotel room this day. Whenever we could afford to, we got away from his aunt's house to have our own private time. This was one of these days. Relaxed and enjoying the comfort of the hotel room, he stretched out on the bed and started singing that song when the video came on. At first, I lay across the bed, pretending it was all swell. But I decided to sit up. I smiled. I had to make him feel comfortable as if I was truly unaffected by his somewhat of an admission. He smiled back, obviously feeling like his secret was a joke. I didn't find it funny.

After he finished singing, I asked. "You did it, didn't you? You may as well tell me the truth. I mean I already know. It's old and it really doesn't matter. I'll just feel better if you'd be honest about it. You may as well man up."

That completely wiped that jokester smile from his face. He got up and sat on the full-sized bed directly across from me. I had him exactly where I wanted him. He lifted his head and looked at me. He came to the corner of the bed where I sat and kneeled on the floor between my legs, his head hung low.

After a few moments, he looked up and said, "Yes, I did it."

I couldn't tell you how my hand did its own thing. That wasn't supposed to be my reaction. I smacked straight to the floor the hell he hid behind his face.

"Now tell me what happened!" I had every right to know. If he was bad enough to screw that whore in my house, he should've been man enough to tell me what happened. "What happened?" I screamed at him again because he started pleading with me not to do this. I wouldn't have any of that. I needed to know just how she seduced him into being disrespectful and disloyal to me. I deserved that, and he was going to give it to me.

He said she came to the house one day to buy work. "I was feeling bad because I needed dope. She was getting ready to leave when I asked her if she knew where I could get some. She told she had some on her if I wanted some. That's how it started. She started coming over all the time. When she came, she bought dope, weed, and pills, knowing that's my weakness. I let her in every time. We were sitting in the living room on the sofa high one night. She slid over to me, and unbuckled and unzipped my pants. She pulled it out and put it in her mouth and started to blow me. When she was done, she stood up and started taking off her clothes. Then she sat on me and rode me."

I cut him off. I know he was giving me what I asked, but damn! It was way too much for me to handle. I like to think that when I had something, it was mine and no one else was entitled to it. And if someone else got to it, it's now a tainted thing nobody wants. It made me think back on Sonja. She was always loose. She even had a major crush on her sister's husband and slept with her own aunt's husband. Even worse, she did it in her aunt's house while she stayed with them. I couldn't explain how I could look over that and stayed her friend, maybe because we went through a hard time together as kids. No one wants to believe their best friend would stab them in the back.

No matter how bad it sounded, I wasn't done with Marcus. Since he got what he wanted, I needed to know if it was worth it. So, I asked him.

"Did it feel good, nigga? Did you cum, you trick?" I wasn't being nice, but he betrayed me in my own house. He didn't deserve kindness.

He told me it wasn't worth it, and that he didn't bust a nut either.

"Why? That makes no sense."

"I just started to feel bad and made her get off me."

I smacked him again. This time with my disrespectful back hand. I couldn't control it. My reflexes were in full effect that day. I was vexed, enraged, and infuriated times infinity. "You mean to tell me you sexed that whore and you didn't cum. You expect me to believe that?"

He really thought I was dumb. I guess after everything he was allowed to do to me, I showed him I was. How could he really expect me to believe in the heat of the moment he thought of me, and that suddenly he felt bad enough to put her out? Well, at least he confessed to screwing my best friend.

We spent the rest of the night in silence. I didn't allow him to touch me in anyway, and I had no more words for him. He sat on the other bed in another world, somewhere high. Me, I stared him down until I fell asleep, regretting the day I met him at the service station.

He managed to hang on to a little drug package. Every day he'd catch rides to and from where he hung to get his hustle off. I had no life at this point. I sat in the house all day, every day, with nothing much to do. I'd call my children every day, and talking to them gave me moments of happiness. I had to somehow get the life back where I could be with them, although I had nothing to work with.

My boys told me my mother had been in contact. CeQuan gave me her number and I wrote it down. I didn't call her right away, and I'm not sure why not. But just a few days later I called. She told me she was working a full-time construction job but still using. I was disappointed. I hoped she'd be able to help me, but why would I hope that? She never gave me any cause to believe she'd be in good enough of a place to help. I was on my own, and I would have to get out of this hole alone.

CHAPTER 13

A DIFFERENT HUSTLE

MARCUS AND I DECIDED WE HAD INTRUDED ON HIS AUNT long enough, so we left her house for good. We were officially homeless. We stayed at hotels whenever we could, but most days we couldn't, so we hung out with Marcus's other relatives. They lived across town on the west side, where Marcus used to hang when I first met him. I was now regularly speaking with my mom, who gave me money every time she got paid. But I could never hold on to anything. Marcus took everything, even what my mother gave me. I couldn't complain though. It allowed Marcus to buy bigger bits of drugs to sell and keep us afloat. But with two dope habits, no amount of money was enough.

My mom told me one day she bumped into my dad's sister and she got his number from her. I wasn't sure why that concerned me. As far as I was concerned, he was a complete stranger to me. I hadn't seen or heard from that man since I was a little girl. He just stopped showing up to get me one day and I hadn't seen him since. I was eight. Mom said maybe he would be better able to help me, so I wrote down his number. I didn't know if I'd call, and if I did, what I'd say. Would I tell him I was a homeless dope head and had a good-for-nothing boyfriend that was the cause of everything? Part of me wanted to call him because I needed to get away. But I didn't want to impose on anyone unless I really couldn't find a way to get by on my own.

Marcus's relatives were cool. They were a couple of cousins who were also addicted to heroin. They were older than both Marcus and me but still living at home with their mother. She was a single parent and knew about their drug use as well as ours. She'd sometimes offer us her place to stay and feed us. Most times, we were there without her knowing. That secretly had become our home too.

Things looked bad for us. We had no plans for our young lives or our futures. We just lived day to day. I started going with Marcus on the block to make sells. But like everything else that had fallen apart, that was short-lived. We were in too deep. Flat broke, I soon found it all too unbearable. I told Marcus I was going to call my dad and see what he could do.

It was the beginning of summer 2001 when I made that call. He was excited to hear from the baby girl he abandoned at eight years old. We talked for a while, catching up on things we missed all these years. I learned that I had a younger brother, who also lived in DC. They lived separately because he was no longer with his mom. I told my dad about Marcus and that I had been arrested for selling drugs and lost my place while I was incarcerated. I had to be honest with that part of my life. There was no other way to explain my homelessness. But I couldn't bring myself to tell him the entire truth—that I was an addict.

Marcus sat and listened in silence while I spoke on the phone. I was happy when my dad asked me the question I hoped he would.

"How do you feel about coming to DC to live with me? I have a couple of businesses that you and Marcus could help me run."

I accepted the offer right away. He said in two days, on Friday, he'd come down and pick us up. I felt the deepest sense of relief than I had felt in a long time. I would have a home to stay, finally. I wish in that moment I had wised up and gone to DC alone, leaving Marcus behind for good. But I didn't think of that. I only thought about how Marcus and I needed to get enough dope for our time in DC. We racked our brains trying to figure it out, and Marcus came up with a brilliant idea for how we could get money.

He told me he was going to get his homeboy to take him to the mall that day. He would boost clothes he knew were hot on the street, the expensive named brands all drug dealers liked to wear. In less than thirty minutes his ride pulled up. Just like that, he was on his way to the mall. I sat eagerly at his family's house waiting for him to get back.

Around two hours later, he walked back through the door. The smile on his face put one on mine. He grabbed my hand and led me up the stairs. Closing and locking the door behind us, he pulled a little knot of money out of his pocket, flashing what he earned. I never knew how good Ben Franklin could look to me. He took a twenty from under him and slid the rest back in his pocket. From his little fifth pocket, he pulled out heroin. I was all smiles. He had come through for us. I asked him how much money he made off the clothes. He smiled and, pulling out weed and a blunt, said he made $350. Three hundred and fifty in two hours! We both sniffed huge amounts of dope, then he rolled the blunt. We celebrated by getting high. It was a special night, because we had gone days without being high. Only having enough dope between the two of us to keep the sickness off. Now we had more than enough.

The following afternoon, Marcus's people took us both to the mall. I was no thief. But I thought the more money, the better. That day I was willing to learn.

Marcus put on an oversized coat, and I put on one too. He explained to me that was his method for stealing. It was an easier and better way to get more things. On our way, I listened attentively to Marcus's tips on how to steal. We were going to DC in the morning and needed twice the money he got the day before to get enough dope for the two of us. I listened to every word of advice and remembered not to look suspect.

As we approached the store he reminded me again. "Two minutes. We're only going to be in there for two minutes. As soon as we get in the store, split up. You go your way and I'll go mine. Grab whatever you can and make sure there's no alarms. If you're scared and feel like you're being watched, just go back to the car and wait for me. Don't keep stealing. I know what I'm doing, but you don't. So, don't get caught."

As soon as we walked in I got nervous. I thought about how stupid we must've looked with big coats on in the summer time. He headed to the men's section and I to the women's section. "Two minutes" was the refrain I played over and over in my head as I grabbed the best name-brand clothing. After I looked around to make sure there were no alarms, I rushed toward the women's fitting room and wasted no time stuffing my oversized coat with everything I retrieved from the floor. Two minutes, two minutes. My heart skipped beats, and my stomach churned.

The only time I'd ever felt that way was in court. I had no other choice but to face whatever that might face me on the other side of the fitting room. I rushed out with hopes of escape and meeting Marcus back at the car.

Successfully out the store, I ran for my freedom. All my anxiety went away the moment I noticed Marcus in the front seat. The car was already started when I jumped in and we pulled off. I felt safe and unstoppable. That was a rush I wouldn't mind having again. I unzipped my coat and began pulling out the stolen merchandise. From the front seat, Marcus watched. I saw dollar signs in his eyes. He was impressed with my success as a first-timer. It totaled $500. Marcus reached over the seat, handing me his big bag full of merchandise. His totaled $600 when I added it up. Between the two of us we had $1,100 dollars, and half of that we got to put in our pockets to take to DC. We all were happy, including the driver. And so, our new hustle was formed.

Marcus's people knew of a couple of spots around town where neighborhood drug dealers hung and took us there. Those guys had no problem paying half price for those expensive clothing. Even better, they were eager to find out when we would be back with more. But we couldn't make promises since we were leaving Virginia the next morning. We made $550 that day. We gave his people eighty dollars for helping us out with everything. We still had $200 of what Marcus made the day before, which we used on dope. We were all set for DC.

My dad showed up bright and early the next morning, after we got our sickness off. He stood outside by his big, old-school van, eager to meet his daughter. I was out of the house before Marcus. I walked toward Dad and he gave me the biggest hug ever. His big wide smile made me give one right back. I couldn't help but stare at that gap, where his missing tooth was, front and center of his mouth when he told me I was beautiful. He told me I looked just like my mother when she was younger. I disagreed. I looked nothing like her. Neither did I look anything like that funny-looking, darker-complexioned man who stood in front of me. I don't think he thought about that missing tooth when he smiled. I walked over to his girlfriend. I bet she thought I was smiling at her. Truthfully, I smiled at the silly thought I was having about his tooth.

She greeted me with a hug just like my dad. Tight, as if she had known me for a while. When I pulled back from her embrace, she grabbed my face and asked if I was really his daughter.

"What? What kind of question is that?"

She quickly explained I was way too pretty to have come from him.

We all laughed. They didn't know I was laughing in agreement. Was Mom sure that he was my dad? Or was he just one of her encounters that she chose to be my dad?

Marcus grabbed all of our attention when he came out of the house. Just like with me, my dad greeted him with a hug. After loading our bags, we all piled into my dad's van. He asked us if we wanted something to eat before we got on 95. Even his girlfriend must have been hungry because we all said yes.

We all ordered waffles, eggs, and bacon while we sat and got acquainted. I had so many questions for my dad but now wasn't the right time. I needed the two of us alone, in privacy, before I grilled him. So, we kept our conversation light but I mostly let him lead. I followed right up with answers to his questions and our conversation just flowed.

"So, how are your mother and aunts and stuff doing?" He was so country, sounding like he'd come out of a hillbilly farm somewhere.

"They're doing alright," I answered, not feeling up to going into details.

"What about your grandmother? Is she still with that crazy nigga? Yeah, I heard about what he did to your uncle too. I don't see how she's still with him after what he did to your mom and them. I wanted to kick his you-know-what back in the day." He ranted on, one thing right after another. I was shocked to know he knew so much of what happened when my mother was young. They caught hell. And to think of it, I think they must have been crazy because of what they went through.

We finished our breakfast rather quickly and hit the road. I was still sleepy and slept through our ride to DC. I woke up to my dad calling my name. I looked at his dashboard. If that old clock was right, it was almost noon when we were pulling up to his neighborhood.

I don't know what I expected, but that place looked rough. I saw no regular apartment complexes like I was used to in Richmond. In Hilltop,

Ruffin Rd, or almost anywhere else I lived in Richmond, the apartment buildings were almost like townhouses, all connected together but each had its own entrance. Here in DC, one large building housed hundreds of apartment units.

I frowned at this run-down place. It was nothing like I wanted. The interior of the building was no different. I hated it. But the truth was I had no grounds to complain. I was homeless and should've been grateful to have any roof over my head. My dad took time out of his day to come all the way down to rescue me from the streets. So, I made up in my mind that I'd adjust to it. No matter how much I disliked it, I'd learn to love it. I was going to put on my grateful hat.

The apartment was worse than that old van he drove. There was absolutely no life in it, as if it were unoccupied or used for storage. But even my storage wouldn't look like this. It was badly in need of a makeover. There was not a single picture on the walls. No curtains. No color. Just dead gloom. For the life of me, I couldn't understand how his girlfriend could be okay with it. Maybe she lived somewhere else and he did too? Maybe he was just dropping us off at their storage to give us a place to stay? I didn't know, but I was definitely going to ask my dad when I got him alone.

He gave us a tour of the place. He showed us to one of the rooms and told us it would be ours. There was a mattress and a box spring that sat on the floor. Nothing else filled the space but ugly, old curtains that hung from the window. I wondered if that mattress was clean, who had been on it, and where he'd got it from. But I couldn't bring myself to ask him.

Then he showed us his bedroom, which didn't look different from the previous one. By now, I didn't want to see the bathroom. I figured I already knew what to expect. If I had to use someone's bathroom, I had a terrible habit of pulling their curtain back to check out the tub. If that tub was dirty, I wouldn't use the bathroom. I would just hold it till I made it somewhere else. I had a feeling that here in my dad's apartment I needed the same shower shoes they used down at the jail to take a shower here.

This place looked like it belonged to some sixty-year-old bachelor who didn't care where he lived. It needed love, and maybe I would be the one to fix it all up.

Dad and I left Marcus and Dad's girlfriend in the living room and went to the terrace to talk. I had a conversation for him that he might not have been ready for. Before I could begin, his girlfriend opened the balcony doors and told him someone was there to see him. He told me he'd be right back. While Dad was away, I observed the outside space surrounding the terrace. It didn't look nearly as bad as the front of the place or the hallway.

Maybe it was as bad, or maybe my gratefulness had seeped in. But I no longer felt the disdain that surged when we first pulled up to the house. What filled me instead was a sense of relief, something I hadn't felt in a long time, because I had just been rescued by someone I longed for throughout my troubled childhood. But where was my hero when I needed him to save the day? To liberate me from the abuse I was suffering at the hands of Mom? To set before me a role model to help develop my path, give me direction, tell me to go back to school? To give me a voice of reason? Someone to lean on, depend on, to trust? Or at least to provide the basic needs I needed as a child—food, clothing, shoes, boy talks, or just normal things about life?

Tears started welling up, and I wiped them dry. I couldn't go back in time, so I wouldn't try. What we *could* do now was form the bond we didn't have the chance to establish, one that was different from what I had with Mom, one that would last forever. This could truly be my fresh start. He had shown me that he had my back.

I wanted so badly to tell him the truth about my chemical dependency and how it all started with Marcus. Now I wish I had left Marcus behind, so that I could start anew. Dad deserved to have a daughter who wasn't a user because he was going to provide for me now. I couldn't take advantage of him like that.

"I'm back," said Dad as he shut the terrace door behind him. He kept a smile on his face.

I was anxious to get everything of my chest so I started. "First, let me start by telling you how grateful I am that you are helping me."

He cut me off. "No, no, no. It's only right. You're my daughter. I do owe you that much. I did miss a great deal of your life and I regret it."

"Wyndell, the door!" his girlfriend yelled from the inside of the apartment.

"Hold on one more time, baby girl. I'll be right back."

"Yeah, no hurry. Go ahead." I didn't think twice about these interruptions. I was simply happy how our interactions were so natural. Nothing needed to be rehearsed, and the conversation just flowed. No awkward silence, no talking over each other. We were father and daughter.

"I'm back!" This time Dad returned with a beer in his hand. He sat down and pulled his chair closer to me. "Sorry about that. These people keep bothering me. Now where were we again?" He chuckled at his own self.

"You know I went through hell after you disappeared. Mom started dating this guy that got her hooked onto drugs. They lasted quite a few years until the drugs split them apart, I guess. After he left, Dad, I went through it."

"What do you mean you 'went through it'?" he sat straight up, with a concerned look on his face.

"Mom started abusing me. Beating the hell out of me for stupid reasons. Now that I'm older, I'm guessing it was because she wanted to get high and couldn't. She used to beat me with an extension cord until she drew blood." My eyes got watery as I continued to tell Dad what I went through as a child. I realized the pain was still there as silent tears dripped from my eyes. In telling him, my wounds were reopened. Fresh, new and painful. Still hurting as if the abuse was occurring at that instant.

He listened and watched me with hurt in his eyes. It was a painful story that no real dad wanted to hear that his child suffered. I continued, and gave him some better news. I told him his grandsons were turning eight and five and they lived with their dad, who taught me the streets when I was fourteen. I grew accustomed to street life, and it was as good of a replacement of home life, since Mom wasn't even home that much and wasn't buying food or anything else. I told him I had to drop out of school after I had my son because there was no one to look after him, but the streets encouraged me, pushed me, and gave me direction. I didn't feel like I was doing anything wrong, because it helped me support myself and my children.

I poured my heart out to my dad as he listened intently. But before I told him anything more about me, I felt an urge to know why he disappeared. "Dad, I wonder, though, why did you disappear from my life? It would have been so different if you had stuck around."

"Well," he sighed. "That same nigga who turned your mom out put a gun to my head one weekend when I came to get you."

"What? Why? Why would he do that?"

"Do you remember how I used to come and get you on the weekends?"

I nodded, the memories came rushing back. On those weekends before Dad disappeared on me, he'd come to pick me up and we'd go shopping together. Whatever I wanted, he made sure I had it—dolls, clothes, milkshakes, Pop Tarts. Dad also took me to visit my aunts and uncles, who would put me in their lap and pretended to be shocked with how much I'd grown in one week. "You look just like your daddy!" they'd exclaim. But with Dad's sudden departure from my life, I never saw them again except one or two chance encounters with one of the aunts.

"One weekend I came to get you, and your mom answered the door. She told me to hold on and she'd be right back with you. I naturally thought she was going to get you because it went down the same way every time I came for you. When the door reopened, it was him telling me to get the heck away from around there, because you were his daughter now. He had a gun pointed at my head. He told me how he'd blow my head off if I ever showed face around there again. So, I just turned around and left, deciding it was best for me to stay away. She had a crazy nigga on her hands that I won't try to deal with. She should've checked him. It wasn't my place to do it. It would've ended up ugly if I did. Not long after that I moved to DC to keep my distance."

I couldn't believe the story I was hearing. Mr. Pete did that? I suddenly felt a rush of hatred for him. But I tried to put him out of my mind. "I often wondered what happened to you," I said to Dad. "I'd stare out of my window and wish you'd show up and take me away from her. I hoped for years, then I stopped hoping and just wondered what happened to you. Now I know. That is crazy." I shook my head in disbelief.

We talked for hours. There was so much to catch up in those fourteen years we spent apart from each other. Dad told me he was a businessman. He had a junkyard where he fixed and sold cars.

"Wyndell, the door again!" his girlfriend interrupted us for the third time.

"I'll be right back, sweet pea," he said to me.

Sweet pea. I smiled at the name. This time he was gone a bit longer, and before he returned Marcus came out to the terrace. He saw the people who came to the door all afternoon, and he told me my dad was a hustler. I thought he was stupid. I didn't believe him.

"Why would you say that? What's gotten into you?"

"I saw the people at the door. They were all junkies." Marcus said Dad gave them something after they gave him money, only he couldn't see what it was Dad gave them.

After trying to convince me Dad was a hustler, he shifted the topic. "Y'all been out here for a while. What are y'all talking about?"

"Not much. Just catching up on everything."

Marcus didn't know that I hadn't seen my dad since I was eight. I never felt like it was something important I needed to talk about, so I never mentioned it, not even after I called Dad up when we were still in Richmond. The extent of Marcus's knowledge about Dad was that he was my dad.

Dad came out to the terrace finally. "Do y'all want something to eat? I want to order a pizza or something."

"Yes! I'm starving," I answered. Plus, my back was starting to hurt. "Dad, we'll be right back." Then I signaled Marcus to the backroom to get a couple sniffs of my medicine. After that, we joined dad back on the patio.

"What kind of pizza do y'all want?" he asked while on the phone with the pizza store.

"Fully loaded with everything," I said.

"Alright, how about hot wings and something to drink?"

We told Dad anything would be fine. I couldn't wait for him to get off the phone—I wanted to know the truth, if he was a hustler. I had told him my part of the story, though not all of it.

When he got off the phone, I told him I had a question to ask him. He smiled at me and said, "Alright, shoot."

"Um, I've been noticing how we were constantly interrupted while we were talking. How different people just keep coming to your door nonstop. Do you sell drugs or something?" I was straight to the point. We were all adults capable of holding adult conversations.

He looked right at Marcus, as if he knew Marcus had spilled the beans. Looking back at me he said, "Come on, let's go in."

We followed him inside and closed the terrace door behind us. He walked over to the kitchen cabinet and opened it. He pulled out from it a large Glad bag full of something. I walked over to get a closer look. Marcus followed me. Inside of the bag were a ton of clear white vials. There was several more bags just like it in the cabinet that were wide open. There were little yellow pills inside the vials that I'd never seen before.

"What are these?" I picked one up and looked at it closely.

He told me they were Ds—Dilaudid. It was heroin in a pill form. He told me they used dope in Virginia, but there, in DC, Ds were popping. He said the dope there was nothing more than a bunch of stepped-on cut. That it was no good compared to these pills. He took one out and held it in his hand, showing Marcus what they looked like. He told us the only way to do those was to shoot them up intravenously. Taking them orally did nothing. He was proud of his hustle. Holding the big bag up, he said, smiling, "They go crazy over these things." He immediately began to school us on the Ds. "I don't sell singles. Each one of these vials holds twelve pills. My people already know not to come with nothing less than $120. This is a part of the business y'all can help me with."

I was shocked to learn that my dad was a hustler, something I had been from a young age. His blood truly ran in my veins. That ambition I had inherited was from him. This was really my chance to bounce back. But my mind immediately shifted to Marcus. I couldn't really bounce back if he continued to hang around. If only I could put him and his $500 something on a bus and shuttle him back to Virginia. I wanted him gone, just like I wanted my dope habit gone.

Dad taught us all about Ds and even introduced us to some of his customers. It was so much to take in, and after the morning's journey, we were all tired. Not even pizza gave us enough energy to stay up any longer. Dad gave us new sheets and a comforter and said good night to us. We waved good night to him, but we weren't about to go to sleep. It was time to get high and nod all night, but we had to be careful because I didn't want Dad to know.

The next morning Marcus and I prepared ourselves for the day Dad had planned. He first took us to his legitimate place of business, his junkyard. It was a huge gated lot full of various vehicles. Some were wrecked, some weren't. There were even a couple of tow trucks in the yard. Dad led us into the trailer he used as his office and showed us around. It wasn't much to for us to see. The space was small and dusty. But I was fascinated by this business-minded man that was my dad. He had both street smarts and business smarts. I could learn a lot from him. Plus, he had money, although looking at him, you'd never be able to tell it. He was very low-key with the life he lived, far from being flashy.

I was different. I had to have the best of everything because Mom gave me nothing. I wanted the best for myself and my children. Everything about me had to shine, and maybe that was where I made my mistake. Being flashy showed everyone I had money, and it cost me. The jealous people reported me to narcotics and landed me in jail. Maybe I wasn't as smart as I thought I was. Some say you can tell when someone got old money. They don't feel the need to be flashy because they are used to their wealth. I wasn't used to it. I was not handed generational wealth or born with a silver spoon in my mouth. I came from struggles, where most black people come from. It's a place where if you're not used to money, you lavish in it when you get it. You want everybody to know you got money. You love the attention. And you get it by wearing fur coats and diamond rings, the best of everything. But at a cost—your life. In one way or another you paid.

I was now ready to get back, in a new city and with my dad, running things the way I was used to. Dad did well with his accomplishments. He rode us around for a few hours introducing us to our new hometown. He said he'd soon buy me a new car for us to get around in. Things were looking brighter, and I felt positive and energetic. After we all grabbed lunch in the busy city, we piled in dad's old van and headed home.

On our second day in DC, we only had a pinch of heroin left. Marcus thought up a way for us to get out the house and find what we needed. He told me to ask Dad if we could use the van to go to the store. I didn't think twice. I got up and headed straight to Dad's room, where he was lying cross the bed and watching sports. Moments later, I walked back to our room holding the keys in my hand and a big smile across my face. It was dope time. We told Dad we'd be right back, and we headed out. Marcus told me if we took longer than expected, I should tell Dad we got lost. I agreed. Marcus got in the driver's seat and I climbed right in the passenger's side. Within minutes we were lost. I never had a good sense of direction, and apparently neither did Marcus.

It's funny how quickly you could find what you wanted in a big new city, if what you are after is drugs, even if you didn't know a soul. It didn't matter we had lost our bearings. Marcus pulled over in a neighborhood that looked way rougher than Dad's. He got out of the car and approached a couple of alcoholics that pointed him in the right direction. Only a block or so from where we pulled over, they said, was where we'd find what we were after. It was trashed and messy, with people on every corner. Kids threw a football back and forth in the midst of that rundown block. I stayed in the van while Marcus got out and approached one of the dudes sitting on a wall. He quickly made an exchange with him and hurried back to the van. It was amazing how fast Marcus drove us back home, as if he knew exactly where he was going.

We were only gone a little time as if we really went to the store. Dad was standing in the middle of the living room floor talking to one of his people when we walked back in the house. He held a beer in his hand and he started smiling when he introduced me as his daughter. He was proud. I wondered if he'd still be proud if he knew I was a dope head. I politely smiled and spoke to his friend, but after a few comments I hurried off saying I needed to go to the bathroom. Except I didn't go. I followed Marcus straight into the bedroom and shut the door, locking it. Quickly, Marcus pulled a bill from his pocket and ripped the bag of dope open. It didn't need to be crushed. It fell apart as soon as he opened the baggie. It was soft and white like baby powder. Nothing like the do-do brown hard dope we were used to. We each had a couple of sniffs that did nothing but kept us from being sick.

Every day for the next couple of weeks, we spent time with Dad and found opportunities to sneak out to waste money on garbage dope. We also made money for Dad, who was now leaving the Ds in Marcus's hands while he went to work at the junkyard. Our helped allowed him to be in two places at once and making money both ways. In return, we were paid handsomely for being his second set of hands.

Dad grew fond of Marcus and trusted his loyalty. Just like with me, Marcus charmed Dad. But Dad would soon get the surprise of his life. Despite the money we were being paid generously, the desire for good heroin was getting the best of us. We began discussing going back to Virginia but were clueless of how we'd get there. Desperate for our highs, we tried crushing and sniffing Ds, although Dad already told us it only worked by shooting it up. I'd never forget that day we patiently waited for Dad to get home and request permission to "go to the store."

We both hopped in the van. I was on the passenger side, as usual. It was the first week of August and hot out. Neither of us could take it anymore, and our hunger for dope didn't help. We drove on, riding past the neighborhood that we would see for the last time, that same place that fed us garbage heroin. The red lights couldn't have changed fast enough. I kept looking behind us as if Dad was following. I was nervous. I knew what we were about to do was wrong, but it wasn't enough to stop us. When we saw the first sign of 95, we took that turn and merged into the heavy traffic. We were headed to Virginia, and fast. If I felt bad, I didn't feel bad enough. My addiction made me willing to do anything, evening stabbing Dad deep in his back after he rescued me from homelessness and sheltered us for two months. We stole his car and even some of his money.

After we were at a safe distance from Dad's home, I relaxed and threw my arms in the air, as if I had been released from jail. The reality was, I was putting myself *back* into the prison named drug addiction. That was the prison I could never get out of, and in this prison, where I felt free but was enslaved, nothing mattered more to me than getting high.

As my hands brushed through the top of the car and along the side of the passenger seat, I realized what we had. It was not just a car. We could *sleep* in this van. I told Marcus excitedly, and he was having the same thought. With a new ride and our new hustle, we were ready for Virginia. I couldn't wait to get there. We had close to two grand to relax on and it was now high time for a fix.

When we were back to Richmond, it was late. By dope standards it was. You wouldn't find dope dealers out late at night like the crack dealers were. Having no choice but to wait till the morning, we got a room for an entire week. I don't think I got any sleep. Every hour passed slower than the one before. I was too anxious to feel what I hadn't felt in months. Marcus and I were up and out of the door bright and early the next morning. It was insane how all the dope fiends lined up for their morning fixes, like how people lined up for methadone. Before heading back to the hotel room, we stopped for whatever necessities we needed to last a few days. Then we barricaded ourselves in our room. In three days I don't think he and I said two words to each other. We were like a zombie couple high as hell, lighting cigarette after cigarette.

Our week in the room really felt like a couple days since we were in such a haze. Instead of getting the room for another week, we decided to leave rather than blowing through another thousand dollars. We needed fresh clothes and shoes badly, but that was the farthest thing from our minds. It's odd how easy it was to blow through money with nothing to show for it. Instead of waiting to get all the way low on money to hustle, I suggested this was the time to pick up where we left off. Marcus agreed. We began going to different malls and robbing them blind. No longer were we stealing randomly. We had developed a clientele that requested things they wanted. Some wouldn't have bought the latest fashion if they had to pay the full price at the store, and Marcus and I supplied them the goods at a discount. I should've been embarrassed for stealing and selling stolen merchandise, but blinded by my dope habit, I had no shame in my game. That's the way it is when you're hooked on drugs.

By junkie standard, things were going great for us. We began to expand our thieving wings beyond Richmond. I knew in the back of my mind that it would catch up to us one day, sooner or later, but most of the time I felt unstoppable, and I enjoyed the material comfort that our theft brought us. One time, on our way out of the store, we were both grabbed by the shoulders at the same time. I already knew what it was. It was Judgment Day.

The officer who stopped us was quickly joined by another officer. They separated Marcus and me and took us into different rooms. They told me security alerted police when they noticed us shoplifting on camera, stuffing our oversized coats with as much merchandise as we could. I was caught, red handed. I had no choice but to hand over everything inside my coat. Immediately, they read me my rights and placed me in cuffs. I knew I was stealing and it was wrong, but I wasn't sure it was serious enough to land me in jail yet again.

At the precinct, I was fingerprinted and processed. They charged me with a felony because I had more than $200 worth of merchandise. I went before the magistrate and was given a bond, but I had no one to get me out. I was transported to the jail that night. I hadn't seen Marcus since we were grabbed at the door, but he was the farthest thing from my mind.

Again, away from Marcus, away from our drugs and thievery, I had time by myself to reflect. I felt angry, but this time more with myself than with Marcus. I had known for a long while now that Maurice's warning was right—Marcus would be my downfall. I already told myself I had to leave him behind. But in my stubbornness and foolishness, I stuck with him. And here I was, in jail again. The truth was that not once did Marcus put a gun to my head, forcing me to go along with anything. Not the heroin, not the theft. I was a willing participant in everything we did together. Maybe I felt obligated because he was my man. Even if that were true, I knew how stupid and crazy I was for thinking that. I just thought he loved me, and that was enough. But on the cold floor of the holding cell, I understood that enough was enough. his "love" was not enough.

I was in jail for two months before I finally got hold of Maurice. I told him about my bail and he bonded me out quickly. I left Marcus behind, determined to make him part of my past. I had absolutely no intention of ever talking to him again. It took losing everything for me to finally come to that decision. But now I had made up my mind. It felt good being clean and not having that devil by my side. I was finally able to be in control of my own mind again.

Aunt Janice welcomed me at her place, where I'd stay and get myself together. She had relocated to the north side of town, down the street from my old hood Jackson Ward. Although it was helpful to have a roof over my head, there was a huge hump I had to get over to get things started. I didn't have the resources to better myself—no money, clothing, job, means of transportation, support. Nothing. My dad's van had long been towed from the parking lot at the mall.

Before I could figure out how to support myself and get my life together, I got in touch with Tameca. She was a young lady I met in Colonial Heights jail, who gave me her number before she left. She was the only girl I talked to in jail, and she was just like me, a heroin addict arrested for shoplifting. But she was a kleptomaniac with a long history of stealing. I called her up, and within a few minutes I found out she went straight home and got high, not giving herself a chance to do better. She had told me she was going to be different when she got out of jail. I can't say I was surprised. Doing time didn't change me overnight either.

Although Tameca was using again, I decided to still hang with her because we had similar struggles. She didn't drive but she always had a ride if she needed to get to places. Soon, I found myself back in stores boosting again, only this time with her. Worse, I started back sniffing dope, and my thieving took to another level. I was writing checks. I found myself in stores with shopping carts full of clothing and paying with fake checks. It worked. I was getting away with tons of stuff, writing $800 to $1000 checks. This way, I built the wardrobe I badly needed. I even replenished my entire shoe collection. I was using again, but I looked nothing like when I was with Marcus. I looked nice, or so I thought. I even started getting my hair done. Not in a hair shop, of course, but at least it was done.

Tameca and I were all over the place selling our clothes. We were in the south in a project they call Hillside one day when I ran into Sonja. She shared a project unit with her son's dad and the other two children she had. I was far from excited to see her. I hadn't planned on ever having to cross paths with that chick again.

When we had the chance to talk, I asked her what I needed to know all these years. "Do you ever plan on telling me the truth about you and Marcus? I know it has been years, but I still want to know. I feel like you do owe me that much."

It was a straightforward question, and it wasn't a surprise to her. Sonja and I knew each other since we were kids, and she knew I didn't beat around the bush. I needed to know where was the loyalty that I rightfully expected from my best friend.

Hesitantly, she started to speak, but not before asking several times that I not get mad on her. I understood that she didn't want to get embarrassed in Hillside in broad day light. I reassured her that I was no longer mad. I just needed to know her side of the story after hearing Marcus's side.

"When you were locked up," she began very softly, looking down toward the ground and now looking up at me, "I came by your house to buy coke from Marcus to flip. I had dope that day and he was sick. He asked me if I knew where he could get some. I told him I had some and I'd give him some if he wanted. Then we both sat down and got high. That high turned into an all-day thing. He had weed and I had a couple of pills, and we just zoned. Every day after that, I came to your house and brought dope, pills, and weed. Sometimes liquor. We were sitting in the living room high one night when he asked me to come to your room for a minute. He said he had to show me something. When I got in there he was all over me. He took my shirt off and started kissing me. One thing led to another and we had sex." She hung her head low, looking sheepish.

Her confession provoked something in me. I knew I asked for it, but just like with Marcus, it was too much for me to handle. I asked if it happened more than once. She said yes. Her honesty brought shooting pain right through my chest. It must've taken everything in me not to punch her in her face again. Hearing her side of the story hurt, but not as much as when Marcus gave me his.

"Why?" I asked. "Why were you coming to my place when I wasn't there? And into my bedroom?" I was raising my voice. "Why didn't you just tell him you wouldn't go to my bedroom?" My questions were rhetorical. I only felt the need to ask, but I didn't need answers. I told her real friends don't stab real friends in the back and she was wrong, dead wrong.

Time did heal some, but that day, the wound was opened wide again. Before I left, I told her she was never my real friend and I understood now why my mom always warned me about her.

I believed her story more than Marcus's version. Marcus made it sound like Sonja was the one that came on to him when he was the one who initiated. I remember him telling me on the jail telephone that he was horny. However it happened, they both were wrong. Two guilty parties of the same crime.

I was arrested later that day. One of my tail lights was out and I was pulled over. Instead of giving the cop my name, I gave him Sonja's name, not knowing she was in trouble with the law—suspended license and failure to appear in court. For her offenses, I was placed in a patrol car and taken to Henrico County precinct. There, the process was expeditious, faster than any other precinct I had been in before. I went through the normal procedures of booking before going to see the magistrate. I was nervous. They just fingerprinted me under Sonja. I could only think about what would happen if they found out I had given the cops a false identity, which would get me charged with fraud and no chance of bond.

The magistrate was gracious, granting me a bond of a small sum, only $300. I quickly called a bondsman to get me out. I already had the money in my pocket for bail. I got out before the fingerprints came back.

I was done with Tameca. I'd had enough of stealing and jail. I went straight back to Aunt Janice's after being released. She had recently run into my mom while I was away. She gave me Mom's number and told me Mom wanted me to call. It had been a good while, and I called her the first chance I got.

We talked for what seemed liked hours, and she asked me to come stay with her. I agreed, and I left Aunt Janice's place the following day. She had a great job and was back in church. Her strong faith in God helped her escape the street life she once loved. She was drug free for more than a year strong, and I was proud of her. She shared a place with someone she rented a room from temporarily until she got her own. This area was new to me, although I'd picked up Charlene a few times from here, a run-down area of Blackwell known as Porter Street. It wasn't the cleanest place but I appreciated it. At least I wasn't homeless. I felt a sense of security being back with my mom. I felt "home" again.

Only a few days after I moved there, I met the niece of mom's roommate. Her name was Keisha too. We clicked instantly. Keisha was young and married, with four children and a home. It was a nice four-bedroom home where she wouldn't stay. She left her family for days at a time, preferring the streets because of her addiction. Crack was her thing, and she smoked day and night. We started hanging together a lot, and I never judged her drug use because I too was addicted to a drug.

She introduced me to a different part of Blackwell. There were a lot of street drug dealers. That's where she bought her crack and I got my heroin. She turned tricks with the drug dealers for her drugs. They loved her, or they were in love with that body of hers. Whenever she turned tricks with them, they paid her well for her services. I started back boosting again to afford what I needed. Only a few sheet sets here and there.

"Keisha, can I ask you something?" She asked me on our way back to Mom's spot. "Have you ever smoked coke before?"

I smiled at first. I found the question degrading. In her mind drug addiction was drug addiction, and all kinds of drugs were on the same level. I disagreed with that. I was no crackhead and never had any thoughts of trying it. The closest I came to it was selling it. "No ma'am," I said. "Never thought about it, and never will. I used to sell it, but that's it."

"You should try it. I guarantee you'll like it." Her eyes lit up. "I have an idea. I got a lot of it. Hold on."

We were somewhere on a dirt path in between houses when we stopped. I didn't pay her any attention. It went in one ear and straight out the other. But she started rummaging through her pockets, and then she pulled out her pipe and tore open one of her many baggies of coke. She put the entire rock on that thing and put the fire to the other end.

"What? Are you crazy?" In broad day light she started smoking crack. I frantically looked around to see if there were any police. I couldn't afford an arrest—by now my fingerprints must have come back, and as far as the police department was concerned, I was on the run from the charge of fraud. Keisha didn't even bother looking around before pulling this stunt. She was bold, and that was something else. When I saw there were no police, my focus shifted to her. In all my years of seeing people smoke crack, I never saw anyone hold their smoke long as her.

She took another baggie out her pocket and ripped it open with her teeth. This time she broke the rock in half instead of putting the whole thing on the pipe. She didn't put it to her mouth. She offered it to me. "Here, I'm going to hold it and light it. Just pull and try to hold your smoke for as long as you can."

I didn't object. Although I had always thought that smoking crack was beneath me, I didn't think I had anything to lose by this point. I also didn't think about the consequences of what I was asked to do. So, I did exactly what she said. I put my mouth to the glass stem and pulled until she took the lighter away. I held the smoke for as long as I could, like she told me. She stood there watching to see how I'd react. I let the smoke go and was at first unsure of what I felt. It was just different; that's all I knew. Different from anything I've ever tried. I didn't understand why people were so crazy about that stuff.

We spent the remainder of that day together, and Keisha shared what she got from the dealers. Our day turned into night as we walked. It must have been miles that we walked, talked, and got high. We got back home and continued. Day one turned into day two. Day two turned into day three. The sun had risen and gone down again twice. And on day three I was a girl transformed. It was as if the sun had set and risen on two different people. All morality had gone out of me, and I cared no longer about whatever integrity meant. I was ready to give myself away at a price, a price those same drug dealers Keisha introduced me to were happy to pay. It was easier than boosting and quicker for me to get my fixes and be on my way.

I was a fresh new face on the prostitution scene, not worn out or ran through. This appealed to the young black men that plagued Blackwell's streets with no hopes of a future. A lot of them questioned me. Questions that I was unable to answer. Questions that made me think but did not deter me from what now had become my life. "What are you doing out here like this? You know you're too good for this right?" A guy named Chris asked every time we crossed paths.

I had no answers other than that I was playing the hand I had been dealt. He'd shake his head at me in disappointment.

"Nawh man. I ain't trying to hear that. This ain't you. You're better than this."

Maybe he thought if he kept telling me, it would resonate and get through. He told me almost every day, and although I appreciated his care and persistent encouragement, it didn't change anything. This way of life kept me afloat, because my mom had by now moved to a different location, into a place of her own. I had no knowledge of where Keisha disappeared to. She left without a word. I was alone again and losing weight rapidly as I walked the streets day and night. I refused to sleep for days at a time because my cross addiction had me on a mission. I could have gone to my mom's place, where she'd give me food and a place to rest and shower. But I didn't. I was unwilling to part from the streets that fed me and my ungodly cravings. So I remained in Blackwell, cross-addicted, alone.

CHAPTER 14

TURNING POINT

I WAS A LONER IN A NEW WORLD I KNEW NOTHING ABOUT. IN MY ignorance, I didn't know the full ramifications of my chosen path: cross-addiction, prostitution. A path I chose for myself, or maybe it chose me. Whatever the case, karma found me and served me a piece of what I served up to others. I knew when I hustled that drugs weren't the best thing in the world, although I didn't know just how bad they were. I put these poisons into the hands of people whose lives were valuable, and I helped quicken their ruin. Now my own life was in ruins.

Maybe God brought me into the paths of my former clients to get not just a taste of but a full, real understanding of the fruits of my selfish ambition. I couldn't have learned otherwise what kind of consequences resulted from my greed and pride in wanting the high life. I didn't know why my life turned out this way, but I knew I was lost. I was now a full-fledged street-walking junkie. Not with just one addiction, but two. I got high wherever I could. I now stood for nothing much more than a fix. I didn't even eat much. It wasn't important any more. It only took away from the money I could use to buy drugs.

I did go to Mom's house sometimes, and every time she'd feed me and get me fresh clothes. Never once did she scold me or judge me. She only encouraged me continually and gave me godly advice. Having gone through similar situations, Mom understood fully what kind of strongholds I wrestled with. For many years she too grappled with her love for these demons. But after I showered, ate, and rested up, my footsteps continued in the same direction. I never realized the danger I was putting my life in, as I exposed myself to anyone and everyone.

Nonetheless, day in and day out I was in and out of the cars of strangers, just like my mother was once, prostituting myself for drugs. And it was no different this night when that gray car pulled up beside me.

"Hey, where are you going?" the dark-skinned fella said, slowly driving up next to me. He was wearing a hood, so I could barely see his face in the dark street. "I'm going to pull over right there," he said, pointing toward the curb. "I want you to come here for a minute."

I walked over like he asked. I opened the door to his car and hopped in. He drove off right away while asking me, "So why are you out here?"

I wasn't up for satisfying anyone's curiosity. I was there just for business, and after that they could go their way and I'd go my way, never seeing each other again. So, I didn't answer.

My silence offended him. He grunted and was quiet too, but he quickly turned down a dark street I didn't know was there. There were no residential homes around, or anyone, for that matter. I sat frightened in the car, alone with Satan himself.

After parking the car, he reached across me into his glove compartment and pulled out a gun. Then he took off the bandanna around his neck and covered his mouth with it. Then, angrily, he demanded that I crawl into the back seat. Not putting up a fight, I did what I was told. I wanted to be able to walk away with breath in my lungs. Silent tears started to flow as I sat waiting for him to take his next step.

He opened his door quietly and got out and back inside the backseat. He waved the gun at me and said, "What are you crying for? You don't be out here crying when you're turning tricks with your dumb ass. Jumping in and out of cars with strange niggers."

I was choking up and petrified.

"I'm going to teach your ass a lesson. This should teach you not to jump in and out of cars with strangers."

I knew he was right that what I'd been doing was wrong, but it didn't help ease my fear.

"Take your pants off," he started instructing me.

Not putting up a fight, I did just that.

"Now listen, if you do everything I say you might just walk away from here, but I'm telling you now, if you try something crazy I'm going to blow your head off. Try me."

I did everything he said, with tears streaming down my face nonstop. Then he told me to lie on my back and open my legs while he slid on a condom. "I know you can open your legs wider than that. I don't have all night. Stop playing with me. Let's get this over with."

I opened my legs as wide as I could. He jumped on top and proceeded to do his business with aggression, all the while holding the gun in his hand. In one moment, when I could muster the courage to look at him, he looked emotionless as he took what he wanted from me. But even that he wouldn't allow me. "Turn your head! Don't look at me."

He proceeded to call me every disrespectful name he could think of, on top of what he was already doing to me. I felt worse than I'd ever felt before. Worse than trash. Worse than dirt. Worse than the filthiest thing I'd seen. He finally stopped because he'd ejaculated.

"Hurry up, pull up your pants!" He screamed.

I don't think I could've moved any faster. I wanted to be out of there as quickly as possible.

He gave me one final instruction. "Get your nasty ass out my car and keep walking. If you look back I'm going to blow your head off." That was a warning he didn't have to say twice.

I opened the door and fell out the car trying to get away from him. I stood to my feet, walking fast as I could as I fixed my clothes. I was happy to escape death with my life, but I needed a fast fix to steady myself. A pill of dope and some crack. The traumatic experience wasn't enough to keep me from walking the streets. All I needed was medicine to make the pain and shock all go away. I hadn't learned the lesson my rapist tried to teach me.

After going to my mother's place to wash off everything, I went out again. I stayed on a mission for four days that time. No food, only a snack here and there. On this mission, a catch phrase came to me, and I found comfort in it. I repeated it, believing that what I was going through was only temporary. "You better catch me while you can, like the Gingerbread Man," I said to myself. This was only temporary because God saw it fit to allow me to go through this, and He would bring me out of it. I didn't believe God had given up on me, and I knew that was how I still had hope in the midst of my storm, a storm so severe and so dark that no light beside the light of God could shine through.

"You better catch me while you can, like the Gingerbread Man." I started saying the mantra to myself all the time. It made me believe my street-walking life would soon end. When a man took advantage of me, I said the mantra to myself quietly. I was a young girl lost in a world she hadn't figured out, but I would not be lost forever. My mother stayed in prayer for me. She hadn't given up on me, and neither had God.

After my stints, I went back to Mom's place, and I'd wash up and sleep for a long time. One of these times, I slept away the entire day, only to be awakened by Mom.

"Kee, wake up! Wake up! Look at this!" she shook me and pointed at the TV. It was live broadcast of planes flying into the Twin Towers.

The world has gone mad, I thought. We watched in silence and shook our heads. When the screen switched over to the news anchors, I began to feel sharp pains shoot cross my back. I tried to bear it as I talked to my mother. I didn't want her to know I was not well. But I was also feeling hot, then cold, then hot, then cold. Finally, I began to tremble and I couldn't take it any longer. I got up and headed to the bathroom, not forgetting to take my pants with me. My medicine was in those pockets, as well as the only dollar to my name.

I shut the bathroom door and sat down on the toilet, still shivering. Quickly, I pulled the money and dope from my pocket and crushed up both pills. I never needed more than one. But that day my greed told me one wouldn't do. I did almost three times of what was normal for me. That stuff tasted disgusting, but with the drips of water I sniffed afterwards and a few moments, I'd be well and high. It was complete silence in the bathroom. I zoned immediately and everything went blank. I was stuck, unable to move. I remained conscious, but I couldn't do anything. I could hear but I couldn't see. Then the floor jumped up and smacked my face. I no longer heard anything. And I flat-lined. Then I heard a faint voice call out from somewhere.

"Keisha? Keisha! Open the door!"

It sounded so distant, so far away. I heard it, but I couldn't move. I lay on the floor, somewhere in between heaven and earth, with total loss of control of my body. I wasn't sure if I'd ever return.

Mother's voice grew closer.

"Keisha! What happened?" She was now kneeling in front of me. She began praying for my life, fighting for my life with the Sword, the Word of God.

"I know Lord God, you said you give life and you take it. But I'm asking that you spare my daughter. You gave her to me. It is only because of your mercy she's still here. You told me that the effectual fervent prayers of the righteous avails much. That your eyes are on the righteous, and your ears are attentive to our prayers. You tell us to have no fellowship with the unfruitful works of darkness. Unlike before, I'm listening to your voice and I ask that you listen to mine. You said that you have given us power and authority through Jesus the Christ, my Lord and Savior. I speak to death. You shall not prevail. No weapon formed against us shall prosper. That's what you said, Lord. I know you are a God that shall not lie. You are an Almighty and perfect God. Powerful you are. Nothing or no one compares to you. To you I dedicate my life. For you I live and for you I die. So I say your words in faith, trusting and believing that you will honor my prayer request. My faith makes me believe what you tell me. In the name of Jesus the Christ I ask these things. I speak life and not death into my daughter."

I could hear her. Loudly and more clearly than ever before. She remained so calm, and her voice was so comforting. She who gave life to me was bringing me back from a faraway place, back home, where I belonged.

I opened my eyes.

She had a strength I never knew she possessed, and she sat me up. She cried many tears of joy that I was spared from death, only because God was merciful.

"Thank you, Lord!" she said as she squeezed me. She asked me if I realized what happened.

I told her all I knew was that I was "stuck" when I hit the floor. That was the last thing I remembered.

"You need to get your life together, young lady. That was too close of a call. I almost lost you if it weren't for the grace of God." She shook her head, still shocked but relieved at the same time.

I stayed in the house for the rest of the day, until Mom left me for work. Obstinate, I went back on the streets and gambled with my life.

But still, somewhere in me a tiny voice yelped hope. A hope that I clung on to. A hope that reminded me, "They better catch me while they can, like the Gingerbread Man." I continued with climbing in and out of strangers' cars every day, but I couldn't show my mom I hadn't learned my lesson. I chose to leave and not return. I wasn't done yet with this life, no matter how badly she wanted me to be.

One day, I met a nice guy named James. He was a bachelor in his thirties, with a nice crib and a good job. He learned my spots and picked me up frequently. He took a great liking to me and I didn't understand why. Surely he picked up girls all the time, like the other men. It wasn't until he started picking me up and taking me home with him for days at a time that I realized he wanted more for me than I wanted for myself. He gave me money to feed my desires. Enough to keep me out of the streets and be with him. I couldn't wrap my head around his interest in me. Why? He had more than enough potential to get any woman he wanted. There was nothing wrong with him that I could see. It was especially curious since he didn't use drugs.

Countless times he tried talking me into getting my life together. Go into a program even. He'd make love to me as if I were his woman and he felt a profound passion for me. I didn't feel what he felt, even though I knew he cared for me. He'd make some lucky woman happy one day, but that woman wouldn't be me. I wasn't ready to leave it all behind, and even when he promised to take care of me, it didn't compel me to choose that different path. I only felt irritated when he pushed me to make better choices.

I ran into Tina one day, who I met in the city jail. We picked up where we last left things off and became inseparable in no time. She shared a place with her daughters' dad. He worked in construction. I didn't ask why their daughter didn't live with them. I was just happy to have a place to get high. She and I spent our days and nights together on missions. Her boyfriend knew but didn't care. The only thing that mattered to him was that she fed his demons too. He could care less how many penises she sucked.

"You better catch me while you can, like the Gingerbread Man," I'd softly tell the cars that rode past the chance of having me while they could. On our missions, Tina and I gathered up enough money to buy larger quantities of drugs for the night after we were done. She was cross-addicted as I was, but she had me under the impression while incarcerated that dope was her drug of choice. By far was it her only choice. After coming home for the night, for hours we'd sit at that kitchen table and get high. Dope then cocaine. Cocaine then dope.

We got high so much one night it caused pains in my stomach. It was so intense and wouldn't go away. Then I felt like I was going to have diarrhea, so I ran to the bathroom and sat on the toilet, but only urine came out. The pain persisted, so I continued to sit on the toilet. Then I heard something softly hit the water, but I didn't feel anything leaving my rectum. I knew I wasn't that high. I grabbed some tissue to wipe myself, first though, I took a look.

I screamed, and it must have scared the life out of Tina. She came into the bathroom faster than lightning.

"What's wrong? You alright?"

I couldn't answer. I continued looking at the thing that was hanging between my legs. It was long, gray, and slimy-looking. It looked like a formless creature, and I was completely petrified.

"Let me see. Here, girl, let me have a look."

By now my dignity was the least of my concerns. I opened my legs wider for Tina to see.

"Girl, you're having a miscarriage. I'll call the ambulance." I'm not sure how she was so sure, but her confidence calmed me down.

I didn't even know I was pregnant, and there was no way I could care for the baby if it survived. Could it ever be healthy? I had been high all this time. Did James try to get me pregnant on purpose? Was this his way of keeping me around? Maybe I should try contacting him, although he might not he believe that this was his baby. Sure, I was climbing in and out of cars every day, but both James and I were crazy enough to gamble with our lives and skip the protection.

I couldn't move and remained on the toilet while my mind raced through these questions. Tina was only helpful for the few seconds she was on the phone with 911, after which she went promptly back to the kitchen table to smoke. But very quickly EMT arrived.

"Ma'am, are you okay?" A man squatted down next to me and asked loudly as if he thought I was elderly or part deaf.

"Yes, I'm okay and I can hear."

"We got a call saying you were miscarrying. Do you mind if I have a look?"

I nodded, giving him permission to examine me.

"Yep, she's having a miscarriage. We'd better get her to the ER quick," he told his partner. He turned back to me and asked, "Ma'am, how far along are you?"

I didn't even know I was pregnant. I took a guess and told him around four months. I wondered if they could tell I was an addict or that I was high.

"We brought the stretcher with us just in case we needed it. Turns out we do. Which hospital did you want to go to?"

"Chippenham," I said, since we were already on the Southside, and that was always where I went if I needed to go to a hospital. They helped me off the toilet onto the stretcher. In a short time, I was at the ER. I wasn't in pain at all, though. Maybe I was and my body was too numb from all the narcotics. After all, the narcotics had kept me numb to the pain of my reality, a reality I wasn't bold enough to face. A reality that made me feel worthless.

At the ER, the doctors were briefed about my condition, then they put me in a temporary room for monitoring. They took my vitals, drew my blood, then began their questions. How old are you? Do you have any other children? Were they vaginal births? Any other miscarriages? Have you had any abortions? Do you use drugs? They took my entire history.

I was truthful with everything except about drug use, which I was too embarrassed to admit. The doctor pulled back the sheet back to examine the formless thing that lay on the bed between my legs. He smeared some ultrasound gel on my stomach and tried to listen for the baby's heartbeat.

There it was! A heartbeat loud and clear—my baby was still alive. But what was I to do with it? I couldn't even take care of my other children; God knows I wasn't ready to be a mother again.

"We're going to transport you to a delivery room to have this baby," the doctor put down the ultrasound device and said with a sense of urgency. "I'm sorry but there is nothing we can do to save this pregnancy. The baby is just too young and the umbilical cord is outside of the cervix. I'm going to give you two shots of medicine. One is an Epidural, a numbing medicine I'm sure you're familiar with. And the other is Picotin, which will induce labor. There's nothing else we can do. I'm sorry," she said again, holding my hand.

Suddenly a surge of emotions rushed up to my throat. I loved this baby, who lay dying in my womb because of my drug use. A baby I suffocated with crack and heroin. I hurt deeply for my unborn child, who didn't stand a chance at life. Maybe it was for the better; it could head directly to heaven instead of being stuck with me on earth. If it were born, I was sure it would have medical problems because of all the drugs in my system during the pregnancy.

I was given the meds and transported to delivery. I lay waiting for my cervix to dilate. In less than ten minutes after I was given Picotin, it kicked in and my stomach grumbled like a rolling thunder. Right away, I had diarrhea right there on the bed, and I pressed the call button frantically to get help. Within seconds, the nurses were in my room. I told them the medicine gave me diarrhea and I pooped myself. One of my nurses reassured me it was a normal reaction to Picotin. Immediately they cleaned me up. Their compassion and sweetness made my suffering more bitter. They chose such a wonderful career, dedicating their lives to helping others, even those like me. I wished at that moment that I had graduated from school and done something with myself. They were lucky not to have chosen my path. I was sure they had homes and cars. Had I graduated from high school and gone to college, I'd probably be set in life by now. I wondered if my nurses could ever understand the kind of struggle I had to live through.

After they washed me down quickly and changed my bed linens, I pooped again. The Picotin and Epidural both had taken away whatever control I had over my body. Everything was numb, not just my legs. I apologized for making them do their jobs all over again, but they kindly said it was okay and not to worry. They cleaned me and gave me a bedpan. As I sat on the edge of the bed to allow them to change the bed sheets, my stomach grumbled again. But before the diarrhea came they sat me on the bedpan, and it all poured out of me into the bedpan. It was as though my guts were releasing themselves. And although I was numb everywhere, somehow I felt the baby moving down my body. I told the nurses it was coming.

Sure enough, he plopped out, into the bedpan. I must've forgotten my legs were numb. I jumped to my feet to get him from the pan. I heard a faint cry from him, and my heart melted instantly. He was tiny, and perfect, so perfect. He was fully developed yet underdeveloped at the same time. The nurses took him and wrapped him in a blanket.

Just like any other birth, they immediately began cleaning him. They helped me back to bed right away, where I was made to lie and relax. I lay anxiously, waiting for my turn to hold my baby. They did everything like they'd normally would. They listened to his heart beat. They weighed him. They even took footprints of his tiny little feet. I listened to his little cry. It was soft. It made me cry, too. I wondered if he was in pain, or if he was simply doing what every newborn did.

After the nurses did what they had to do, they brought him to me. I took him into my arms and stared at this little fella. I unwrapped the blanket just a little to take a look at his legs and feet. They were perfect. Just like his cute little fingers. His nose was perfectly symmetrical and cute as a button. His tiny hairy ears were just the right size. His soft skin was darker than most babies at birth. He was perfect in every way, although he couldn't yet open his eyes. I kissed his forehead and told him I loved him. I was hurting so badly inside as I watched my son, who had been developing inside me but whose life was robbed of him because of my drug use.

"Doctor, are you sure there's nothing you can do to save my baby?" I asked the doctor through my tear-filled eyes. The look on her face told it all, and I looked down at my son. I would trade my life for his. Why couldn't the doctors make that happen? I would do anything to give this perfectly formed baby a chance at life, to meet his brothers, who would love and protect him. To grow up and throw footballs around when his older brothers taught him how to play. To run around the block with other kids. To go to the store with me and share a thing of fries together.

They let me be with him, and I couldn't take my eyes off him. The nurses listened to his heartbeat every twenty minutes or so, expecting it to get slower because he was on borrowed time. Each time they listened to his heartbeat it grew more faint. Faint like the little cry that was the first noise he gave to the world when he came out of my body.

Three hours later, they checked him one final time. He lay in my arms, barely clinging on to life. I asked the nurse to take him because I couldn't bear to have him die in my arms. I got angry seeing the nurse leave the room with my baby. Why should such a defenseless infant have to pay the price for my wrongs? I turned my back and stared at the wall, silently weeping. I cried myself to sleep.

Hours later I was awakened by a different nurse. She asked if I needed pain medication. I did, but nothing they could offer would relieve my pain. What might have worked was the kind of medicine you could only get from the streets. Shortly after I woke up, I got up and checked myself out the hospital in the hospital gown they had given me when they took my clothing from me. I was barefoot because I didn't know where my shoes were, but I didn't care. My only goal now was getting back to Tina's to get fixed.

I hitched a ride minutes after walking away from the hospital. Only a sick disgusting pervert stops for someone in a hospital gown with a wristband. That didn't matter, either. We both were sick, and in our sickness we made an exchange. My body for his money. Afterward, he gave me a ride to my dealer's corner. Gown and all, I was unashamed. My dealer was there waiting for me. He sold me the best of both of my worlds. Afterward, the late night gas station across the street sold me my paraphernalia, everything from crack pipe to lighters. My feet picked up speed when I left the store. I wasn't headed to Tina's any longer, and she didn't know I was out of the hospital anyway. It wasn't that I didn't want to see her. I just didn't want to share the drugs my sick body paid for. I walked and I walked. Quickly. Briefly standing at the top of every street I reached. It wasn't the spot. I had to find a street dim enough where I'd be comfortable getting my sickness off and smoking my coke.

Five streets later I reached it. There was a corner lit by a dim light from a pole that stood alone. No houses. It was perfect. I stood next to the pole and a bit of surface around it where I crushed my heroin. I held in my hands everything that mattered at that moment. It was the best way I knew of escaping the reality I faced. I pounded my heroin on the pole's surface, and then I stuck my nose in it, I needed it all. Dipping with my fingertips wasn't going to be enough. I immediately began assembling my stem the way I loved it. I bit the knot off the little baggie of coke. I didn't bother breaking it into pieces. The entire rock would allow me to travel where I so badly needed to go. The glass stem filled and smothered my lungs with smoke as I held fire to the other end. I was out of breath. I made sure to hold on to my smoke for as long as possible. When I couldn't take it anymore, I exhaled. It all felt better. Everything was gone at once. The thoughts of my dead baby were gone. The thoughts of my disparaging life disappeared. I was where I needed to be.

I looked around and sat down on the ground. I was surrounded by everything dark. There was nothing I could see. I sat still like a dummy, then I got up and, putting one foot in front of the other, I began walking. I vanished into the night, walking, and walking. The day broke just when I made it to Tina's. She didn't know I was out of the hospital, but seeing me in my hospital gown, without any shoes on, she figured it all out.

Days later, I was in a new area. Unintentionally leaving Tina's for good. I got stuck in a crack house on Blackwell's Dinwiddie Street. In between trying to make a sales pitch one day, I heard someone yelling my name. "Keisha, Keisha!" I thought I was hearing things; maybe the combination of drugs had me hallucinating. The voice got louder and clearer as the car approached.

"Keisha, I know you hear me calling you!" the car came to a halt.

I turned around, and when I saw Marcus, I was filled with embarrassment. He was fresh out of jail and looking as good as the first day I met him. But I turned around and ran. I ran as if my life were on the line. He followed right behind me, and he caught up in no time.

He backed me into a wall and began talking to me. I refused to look at him. I was too ashamed. Instead, I covered my face with both my hands.

"What are you doing out here walking around? Don't let me find out you're out here doing what I think you're doing. Look at me. Baby, please look at me."

I removed my hands from my face but still couldn't look at him. My head wore a scarf that covered my nappy hair. It remained hidden under there for weeks at a time. My clothing was dingy and threadbare. My sneakers looked rough and sapped as if they barely clung to my feet. It didn't take a genius to figure out the lifestyle I was living.

"What are you doing out here, Keisha? Man, baby, please. Please don't tell me you let yourself go like this. Doing this to support a habit?" He grabbed my face gently and turned it toward him.

I looked up into his eyes and saw tears. I saw the pain that the sight of my situation caused him.

Kissing my lips, he told me he loved me. I had no words, because I didn't feel what he felt. Neither did I owe him any explanation. Even at my worst, I was happy to have been rid of him. I parted ways with Marcus the day I left jail, hoping to never see him again. I wasn't about to rekindle anything with him. I simply walked away.

* * *

I CONTINUED WALKING the streets, but I was beginning to feel more hopeful. The end of those days when I let go of myself was nearing.

I was approached on the street one day by a strange man. He was a tall, unappealing brother. His melanin was heavy, as though he couldn't escape the hot sun beating down on him.

"I've got a word for you, sister."

I stopped right in my tracks. I had all the time in the world to hear what he had to say.

"God said if you don't get your life together, by this time next year you'll be dead." With that, he said, "God bless you," and politely walked off.

I watched him walk away, unable to move, as though my feet had been glued to the ground. What he said in three quick seconds pierced my soul. He vanished into the sun, and I never saw him again. I tried turning back and continued going my way, one small step at a time. I was shocked. "You better catch me while you can, like the Gingerbread Man," I whispered to myself. What did the man mean? I walked on slowly, looking down.

Then I noticed those raggedy shoes on my feet. It was amazing how those shoes saw me through hell and high water, situations I survived only with the strength God had given me. Even after all that had happened to me, I still had those same shoes on my feet. If God wanted, he could've taken those away, too. But He remained faithful, always by my side, and those shoes were a reminder of his steadfast presence. The storm that persisted in my entire life stayed. It didn't come and go like normal storms do. It stayed and beat down vehemently on the house of a wretched young soul. But even that storm couldn't take away this symbol of God's faithfulness. This wretched young soul had hope, because God hadn't given up on her.

I walked and thought. I thought and I walked. Until I hopped into the car of the stranger that waited patiently for me at the corner. I was in and out of cars till the sun had gone down that day. With my hard-earned money, I went to the crack house where I lay my head and kicked back, getting high the remainder of the night.

The following morning I was at it again. I climbed into a van with a clean-cut family man. He wanted an exchange. My body for his money, even though he wore a ring. There was something different about him. I couldn't explain it. But it made me feel comfortable in his presence. He had flagged me down, like every other guy, and like those who pretended to care, he began with some questions.

"What's your name"?

"My name is Keisha, why?"

"Well, hello Miss Keisha, I'm Walter. Nice to meet you." He smiled. I wondered why he stopped to pick me up.

"You asked why as if it's a strange thing to introduce yourself to someone."

"That's because people usually don't care enough to ask. I mean it's not like you're trying to date me or something."

He smiled gently, and that relaxed me. I felt I could trust him. Maybe he also thought he could talk some sense into me.

"Why are you out here doing this? You're young and attractive; there's got to be something else you'd rather be doing with your life."

I looked at him, unsure if he was making a statement or asking a question. "Do you believe in karma, Mr. Walter?" I wasn't really expecting an answer. I continued before he could answer. "Well, I believe whatever you dish out is what comes back to you. Like a boomerang. I wasn't always this way. As a matter of fact, I've been doing this thing almost three years. Well not *this*, but I've been getting high three years. I can't give you an explanation of how I ended up here. But three years ago, if you told me that I'd be doing this, I would've bet my life that you'd turn out wrong. The only answer I have for you, about why I'm here doing this, is karma. At least that's what makes sense to me. I've dug myself in a hole that I don't know how to get out of. Do I like this hole where I lie like an animal, trying to survive? No. But I don't know what else to do. I don't have anywhere else to go. So, these streets have become my home. They feed me and give me everything I need." I said it all calmly, while tears came rolling down my face. There was an enormous pain inside that I didn't know what to do with except medicate it with drugs.

He listened and shook his head. "Well, today may just be the best day of your life, young lady."

"The best day of my life?"

"Yeah, because I'm a cop," he said, pulling out his badge. "And today is the day that you get a chance at a new beginning. I have to take you downtown."

I didn't resist at all. I almost wanted to thank him. I was ready for a break from the street life. I needed to get away from it, really. I hated it. My feet were tired and I was physically worn out and mentally broken. Transportation into custody meant relief for me.

We arrived very quickly, and within minutes I was in lockup, in queue for the tedious process; for the fourth time I was arrested, booked, and fingerprinted. I wasn't given a bond, since I had missed court before. That was okay. I was transported to the jail very soon, and I found comfort in being protected behind those walls. They were saving my life from the streets that wanted nothing less than my death.

The next few weeks I fought to regain myself. My body was unaccustomed to the lack of heroin, which I had been feeding myself every day. I couldn't sleep, and I was uncomfortable all over. But I fit in the environment like a glove. There was no difference between me and the prostitutes and junkies that filled that place. One thing was different, though—my mind. I was determined this time not to leave there the same person I came in as.

Jail time did make me better, for which I was thankful. I wasn't wrestling with thoughts of dope any longer, and coke never really mattered to me. My mind became clear and free. I was able to think about life, and how I'd put the pieces back together.

I was lost in thoughts one afternoon while sitting on my bunk when I heard the news on the TV. "There was a brutal murder on Richmond's Southside last night. Not one, but two black males were gunned down in front of this home." The reporter pointed to the house behind him. "One of the victims was a resident of this home here on Blackwell's Dinwiddie Street. Initially, authorities said it was a robbery. But they realized the suspects were not robbed and now it appears to be a homicide, carried out execution style. One of the victims had a large amount of cash and drugs on him when he was found. Both victims were pronounced dead at the scene of the crime. One of the residents living there witnessed her son take his last breath."

I took a second, long look at the house that the reporter was pointing at. Yellow tape secured the perimeter, blocking off the surroundings of the crime scene. White sheets covered the lifeless bodies on the ground. They both lay right next to each other as if they were having dialogue when the tragedy occurred. To the left of the reporter was the house I got lost in about a year ago, where I'd sit all day and night, feeding my body poison. The reporter called out the names of the men who lost their lives. My heart sank when I heard one of the names, Fe, my drug dealer.

I didn't want to hear any more of it. I didn't need to. I lay down on my bunk and my thoughts drowned out the gasps and animated discussions around me about the homicide. The people I knew, talked with, spent time with, smoked with, were now nothing more than corpses. If God didn't rescue me through that officer, I too could've been a victim last night. I was so used to going about every day, taking everything for granted and making plans for tomorrow as if I was sure I'd live to see it.

I already knew—and experienced first-hand—that karma had her vengeance. Fe was guilty of killing people with the same poison he served me. The same poison I once served many others. Murder for murder, he paid for his sins with his life. I knew that even when we think we're getting away with something, we'd better think twice. It always catches up to us. You reap what you sow.

My mind drifted to the stranger I met that sunny day, who warned me I'd be dead in a year if I didn't change. It was just about a year ago. I hadn't changed my act, really, but God in his mercy scooped me up from my mess and put me here in jail, away from harm's way. I knew it was no coincidence.

I knew that day for sure, I had become different at that moment. I was no longer a junkie, and I was determined to live a different life. Everything I felt I began putting it on paper, so that the promises I made to myself became my reality. My selfish ways would no longer continue, and I would give my sons a better life. I would be a changed person and be the example to my children that I myself needed as a child. I didn't have it all figured out how I'd accomplish it, but I trusted that God would show the way.

I promised myself that when I got out this time, I was going to make up for everything. But first I had to put my faith in God to deliver me from my demons. I refused to believe that my demons were simply a disease that I had to live with for the rest of my life. Not me! I trusted God to deliver me totally, and the only time I'd think back on my old life was when I would give my testimony of victory over these demons, a testimony I was sure I would share and continue sharing one day.

Day and night, I prayed. I never went to church consistently growing up, and the few things I knew about God was what Sister taught me and what I remembered from the odd times Mom took me to church with her. I didn't know very clearly who God was, what He had to do with my life, or how to pray. But there was nowhere else I could turn, so I prayed, using what little knowledge I had from my limited experience with church.

First thing in the morning and last thing at night, I fell to my knees pleading with God for my life. "Dear Father, I repent of all of my sins and I ask that you forgive me, in the name of Jesus Christ. I'm lost. I don't know what else to do. I have nowhere to go, nowhere else to turn. I need your help. I don't know where to begin. If I don't know anything else, I know that I don't want to leave here the same person I came in as. I'm tired. I need your strength because I'm weak and I refuse to be weak anymore. I ask that you take the desire for drugs away from me. Take the craving for heroin off of my lips. Take the taste of cocaine out of my mouth. I don't want it anymore. *Please, Father, please*! I beg you to help me! To give me strength that I can't get from anyone but you. If I can't trust or believe anything else, I know I can trust and believe you. I have faith enough to believe that you can do all things. I know you can. So please, God, do this for me, in the name of Jesus the Christ I pray, Amen."

Daily I cried out to the God. My faith increased each time I fell on my knees. Soon, I developed a hate for the once desirable drugs that destroyed my life. I no longer could see how anyone could love something that drive them only toward ruin. Drug was no longer an option for me. I didn't need a program. So many others attended programs, proclaimed themselves clean, only to relapse right after their probationary time was served. My faith was bigger and stronger than that. I refused to believe the popular persuasions that addiction was a disease that had to be kept at bay, subdued by attending meetings week after week.

Years later, today I still believe that calling addiction a disease only destroys the minds of the weak. It gives people a reason to turn back to their indulgence. I've learned that we have a choice to make, to choose which desires we indulge. Is it going to be the demons? Or is it going to be good, constructive desires? When I thought of addiction as a disease, I only felt fear. Could it be cured? How did they treat it? But when I knew that I had a choice to make, that empowered me. It gave me strength.

During the weeks and months in jail, my faith strengthened. I was a totally different person from the woman who was brought in. My struggle was over, and it was time to build again.

CHAPTER 15

A NEW DAWN

I DID A TOTAL OF EIGHTEEN MONTHS THAT LAST TIME, AND IT transformed me.

When I stood in the holding cell waiting to be released that day, I wasn't scared. I was only excited about the new life ahead. In March 2004, I embraced freedom from my jail sentence, and freedom from those demonic strongholds that tore my life to pieces.

The first thing on my agenda was to get to my children. I needed to hold them and tell them that Mom was back and never leaving again, that I was sorry for being the bad mom I had been to them. My boys, CeQuan and Ketwan, were now eleven and eight. I had missed so much of their life. School, birthdays, everything. But I promised myself I'd make it all up.

"Johnson, open gate one!" the deputy said to her coworker, bringing me back to reality. She stood in front of my cell with my belongings in hand. The powered cell bars slowly moved back. Looking at me, she said, "I know you're happy. Here's your things. I don't want to see you back here again." She gave me a little brown bag containing only a belt and papers, and then she walked me to the door and told me I was free to go.

I took a few steps. I was walking toward freedom, and a new dawn. It had taken so much for me to come to this point.

Outside, I felt the sun I hadn't felt in eighteen months. Liberated. I was completely liberated, and it was the best feeling ever. I could truly tell you how good it felt to be set free from both jail and the demons that took me on a ride the last three years of my life. I turned to look at the jail. I thanked the old building that rescued me. Looking to my left and then my right, I then glanced at the raggedy shoes that enclosed my feet.

The same pair of shoes that God kept on my feet through the hell that I lived in. I didn't know exactly where I'd go from there, but I knew I wasn't turning back to the life God freed me from. With my little brown bag in hand, my feet began to pick up pace. I walked and walked until I ended up at Jay's house, eight miles from jail.

I knocked, anxious to see my boys. Just seconds later, CeQuan, my eldest, opened the door.

"Mom, where have you been? I'm so happy to see you!" His eyes lit up with surprise, and he gave me a long hug. "Where have you been, ma? We haven't heard from you in a long time. I miss you so much."

His innocence and love for me brought tears to my eyes. I was prepared to answer mostly every question he had, but I first needed to see my younger son, Ketwan, who wasn't quite four when I left them. "I know, baby, we're going to talk in a minute. I need to see your brother first. Is he around?"

I remembered Ketwan looking like a three-year-old Jay when I saw him last. Such the cutie pie with his super bowed legs and lisp speech. I can't tell you how cute it was when I held him in my arms and he'd tell me how pretty I was. I'd laugh when he told me that because his lisp got in the way of the "p" in "pretty." I thought of those moments, and moments of CeQuan's birth and birthday parties, when I was away from them. I couldn't imagine what that three-year-old looked like now as an eight-year-old boy.

While I eagerly waited for Ketwan to come out of the bathroom, Jay's mom came and hugged me. She said I looked well and that she was happy to see me. We talked for a moment just like the old times, and in walked my baby boy. No longer was he that short three-year-old whose legs were bent like a bow. He was still cute as ever but his legs straightened a tad bit. He dived into my arms. I felt like he was home. I closed my eyes, holding him close to my heart and imagining him at three before I left. My heart melted. I loved him to pieces, as I loved CeQuan. They were my life. But I had missed so much. I missed Ketwan's first years of school. With everything in me, I promised myself again I was going to make up for what I lost. I couldn't get back the time, but from now on I'd be the mother they needed me to be and provide for all their needs.

Before leaving me to my boys, Jay's mom invited me to spend the night. I was happy she did because I had no idea where else I would go. I sat my boys down to talk to them. I told them I had been in jail for drugs. To my surprise, CeQuan knew. He told me he remembered everything. I didn't have it in me to give them all the details. Plus, they were too young to understand what being hooked on drugs meant.

We talked the day away without even realizing it. They told me Jay was doing ten years in the federal penitentiary and he had been down only a year. While I was still processing that news, CeQuan said, "Mom, you need a job, you can't sell drugs anymore because we need you here. Dad is already doing time. You can't go back there too."

I looked at them both with a serious look on my face. "Sweetheart, that won't happen again. I promise. You have nothing to worry about. That is all past me. I left it all far, far, far behind. I will be here, I promise." I rubbed their cheeks. "I will have a job and you won't have to worry about a thing."

That night, after putting the kids to bed, I lay down and thought about how naïve I was for thinking my children wouldn't know what I was doing or pick it all up. Children learn fast, especially from their own parents. I had to be a different, better mother from now on. I had always loved them both, but now I appreciated more than ever before how precious they were to me. They were God's gift to me, and I had to do what was right. I looked at them while they were asleep, and I told myself I'd do anything to protect them. They were growing up to be young men in a society that wouldn't look favorably upon them, so I had to lead by the best example I could possibly set for them. Their dad now away in prison, it was up to me to show them the right way forward.

Jay's parents offered to let me stay as long as I needed to. And without me asking, Jay's mom gave me money to help me out with clothing and things I needed. I appreciated how they had always been there for me. That had never changed. I wished at that moment I knew where my own mother was, but I had grown accustomed to figuring things out without her.

I began trying to adjust to life with my children at Jay's parents' house. It was a whole new ball game learning my boys all over again. I got to see them off to school and help them with homework. I had to work hard to fight off the urge to dwell on the past and the things I lost. I had to force myself to focus on the present and fully enjoy what I now had with my boys.

Within a few days of my return, Jay's mother gave me a ride to the Department of Motor Vehicles. I had to start with state identification. That was the first step to getting a job or anything else I needed. There I ran into Jalisa, an old school friend of mine. It had been years since I saw her last, and I was excited to see a familiar face. We exchanged numbers and later we caught up with each other right away. I didn't hide from her the fact that I was fresh out of jail or that I had a dope habit before. It didn't matter to her. To her, what mattered was what I was doing in the present. She told me about a job that was hiring where we could both get work. She offered to be my transportation there and back if we both got the job.

A week hadn't gone by before we both received phone calls extending the good news, offering us both a job with the same days and hours. It didn't matter that the job paid us $7.50 an hour, or that the production job required twelve-hour shifts. I also didn't mind the eighteen-mile commute each way. We were grateful because we both were high school dropouts without many other options.

Our first day wasn't too bad. I was given a chance at work so I couldn't complain, even though after the first day I had shooting pains in my feet from standing twelve hours. It would've helped to have better footwear to support my feet, but I was okay without it. Jalisa offered me her place to stay. We both agreed it would be better since it'd save us gas and time.

Although I didn't want to leave my boys, it was imperative that I get back on my feet. I sat them down and explained my plans. They understood and supported me. Parting again was hard for both them and me, but I reassured them that I'd call often. Then, with my bags in hand, I was off, into the direction that could only lead me to good places as a productive, law-abiding citizen.

I hadn't known then all the joys and challenges of beginning a new life. As sweet as my reunion with my children, my challenges were bitter, as someone with a felony record. I was determined that my record was no excuse for failure. I needed to get my boys back and get a place of our own. I needed a car. I needed to be a mom. To accomplish it all, I persisted in finding better jobs. I landed one part-time position in a retail department. I needed more to be able to support my children too.

But the uphill battle was no cake walk. I was turned down everywhere I went. Apartments I applied to. Jobs I applied to. It felt like the world was against me, a felon. The world turned its back on me, as if forcing me back to what landed me with the conviction in the first place.

Eventually I gave in. I started selling cocaine a little. I started selling to my aunt and her friends the same way I used to. But I felt no temptation in the least to use it myself, further convincing me that it was more a choice than a disease. This time, I kept my hustle at a minimum. It didn't last long anyway, since I was working two jobs. It became too much for me to handle, and I made the choice of letting go of the unlawful to continue in the right direction.

Jalisa and I began hitting the clubs regularly after work. I needed it to relax my mind, to get away from the twelve slave hours of the job we worked. I also piled on top of that twenty additional hours every week. These brief times of fun energized me, and I was beginning to come back to my old self before the drug use. I wanted to take care of myself again, have a respectable wardrobe, fix my hair, and look more than just presentable.

I shopped a lot, but I wasn't frivolous with my money, and I didn't shop for just myself. I got things for my boys so that their grandparents only had to provide them a roof. I bought my boys clothing, shoes, trips to the barbershop, school supplies, modest birthday gifts. Things were improving fast, although I was still technically homeless. Where I lay my head at night was my friend's, and she allowed me to stay there out of her kindness. That place wasn't my own, and I couldn't welcome my children to live there with me. I needed to work harder.

* * *

JALISA AND I headed to the club one Friday the way we regularly did. We got sexy the way women do when they want to turn heads, except I couldn't wear the heels after standing on my feet for twelve plus hours.

Besides that, I went all out. My snug name-brand jeans and top revealed my curves, which I loved showing off after I gained them back. My butt and thighs were firm and healthy as ever. My confidence was at full capacity as I took my stride. I was confident not only in my looks, but also in the direction I was headed in life.

I stood in the packed club with Jalisa, looking the way I felt, and we were sipping on a couple of margaritas. It never took much for me since I was never a drinker. Just one martini and I was good. From the side of the floor we watched the entire club scene and danced softly to ourselves. My song came on and I got lost in the music.

Then suddenly I was interrupted.

"Oh my Gosh. I knew it man, I knew it!"

I was bum rushed and kissed on my lips before I could see who kissed me. Then, I found myself in the arms of a stranger. Jalisa stood watching, not about to come sort out the situation for me.

After a few moments, the stranger pulled back from his embrace to let me have a look at him.

It was Chris from Blackwell. The same guy who tried to talk sense into me every time we saw each other, who tried to convince me I was living a life that wasn't mine. His face was so close to mine that I could feel the heat from his breath. And no, it didn't stink.

"I'm so proud of you, man. I'm so proud of you. This is you and you look so dam good. But I knew you would, I knew you would bounce back!" His excitement had me excited. A young lady selling roses was walking by, and Chris stopped her and bought every rose in her hand. He gave them to me and told me he loved me.

It all made me feel special. Not just because of the roses. He was excited to see I was well; he had seen me at my worst and didn't judge me then. I smiled, feeling like a queen. Every woman in the club must've been envious—how often does a girl get roses in a club? He pulled out his cell phone and asked for my number. I gave it to him. He deserved it.

I wasn't quite sure at that point what his intentions were, but I considered him my friend. Even when I felt like I was worthless he never treated me like it. That meant everything to me.

* * *

Over the next couple of months, I continued to provide for my children and make trips to see them when I could find the time. My financial situation improved slightly because I could save. The more I worked, the harder I tried. But having a place of my own still seemed like a distant reality. The application fees were beginning to be too much for nothing.

As I came face to face with the difficulties of my situation, I began to see more and more clearly the foolishness of the decisions I had made. They came with consequences that stuck for a long time, and it would take all of me, and more, to get back in society and survive in it. I had learned my lesson, but society tried its hardest to keep me from growing, denying me gainful work and making sure I'd pay for the mistakes I made. It wasn't enough that I'd done time for my crimes.

I bounced from house to house, friend to friend, sometimes even dragging my children along on the weekends I had them. For the following few years, that was the pattern, and I couldn't emerge from the situation. The projects were my last resort. They too denied me. Was it me? Or was it because of the color of my skin? Why did I feel like I was being punished and subjugated to the point of no return? But I knew I wasn't alone in my struggle. It was the same for most blacks who wanted better for themselves.

My mind became inquisitive. I needed answers to some questions. Not just for me, but for all of my people walking in my shoes. I realized that I couldn't win, no matter how hard I tried, if my oppressors continued to have power over me and if I remained in sin. The more I struggled, the more I questioned, and I was backed into a corner with no answers but turning to God.

That wasn't a bad thing. Maybe backing me into a corner was God's way of getting my attention, again. I learned that all things happen for a reason. Especially when your life has purpose.

To understand my situation and figure a way forward, I started paying attention to my oppressors and how their unjust, despotic ways pushed me into a place of hardship. To emerge from my difficulties, I couldn't waste time on things that didn't matter. I was in the battle of my life. A battle where my children would be affected if I lost, because they weren't just young boys, but black ones. The statistics don't lie. I studied them. Evidence proves that ignorance is likely to beset the minds of fatherless black males. My boys were fatherless in a sense, with Jay doing ten years in the feds. With no male figure showing them the way, and their grandparents were too sweet and oblivious to the streets, the only thing my sons had was peer pressure to influence their way of life. I had to do my best to help prepare them for the world.

But I knew I had to evolve a bit, because I had to be both mother and father to them, but there were things I simply couldn't do as a woman. I remained in constant prayers, asking God to help me be a good mother, who would raise my boys to be upstanding, wise, and knowledgeable young men.

CHAPTER 16

FINDING AND RIPPING OUT THE ROOTS OF UGLINESS

Feeling somewhat weak on my own in the face of all the challenges, I yearned for something. I didn't know what it was, but I began to date, hoping it'd fill the emptiness in my soul. I soon realized that wasn't it. It wasn't at all satisfying to me. Once again, I found myself on my knees day and night in prayer. Only this time, I was in prayer for a husband. Prayer had become my answer for everything. I cut off all contact with male friends except Maurice and Rock. They were still around, having become more like brothers to me. They both had earned a special place in my heart.

There was one other guy who I had become good friends with.

Brandon and I met when I was working at a retail store. He came in one day and just struck up a conversation with me. From there, we quickly became friends. In fact, he was something like a homegirl, my best friend. Brandon was the total opposite of everything I ever desired in a boyfriend. I was far from attracted to him but he was there for me. He was married, living with his wife and two children. I knew he was attracted to me, but I made sure he understood that we could only be friends. In my new life, I wanted only to do the right things. I wouldn't break up the family of a married man.

Even in our friendship, he was way too goofy and talkative. I disliked that about him. He was far more carefree than anyone I've ever known. I didn't care for that either.

Nevertheless, in the short time we became friends, Brandon and I learned a lot about each other. Above all else, I appreciated that he never judged me. He introduced me to his wife in a brief conversation over the phone once. She told me she was comfortable with our friendship and she didn't have a problem with me. I figured out why quickly. Through me she was able to reach Brandon whenever she had trouble finding him—or so she thought. It bothered me and I asked her to stop calling my phone looking for him, that he was her husband, not mine.

Brandon seemed to have a lot of free time on his hands. I never bothered to question his story. I really didn't care because it wasn't my business. He and I were only friends. A year into our friendship, we were closer than ever. We were all over Richmond hanging out like a couple of girls do. I introduced him to my brothers Maurice and Rock, and I even took him around my friends. We hung so tight my people all became familiar with him, but they all knew nothing was there, at least not on my end.

Brandon and I decided to go clubbing one warm summer night. Downtown Richmond's Shockoe Bottom was the hot spot and our choice. The clubs there let out at 2:00 a.m. We were walking to the car and laughing about the fun we had. He unlocked the doors to his car as we approached. We both got in and he cranked the car, ready to pull off.

"Hello Brandon," a low female voice spoke from the back seat. She nearly scared the life out of us. I must've pissed myself.

"What are you doing in here? How'd you get in my car?"

We both turned back toward her. I hadn't met Brandon's wife before that moment. Before I said anything, Brandon and his wife started.

"Why aren't you at work? What are you doing in my car?" Brandon asked.

"Don't worry about all of that. The more important question is why you're never at home and what you're doing out here with her." She was dressed in her work uniform. She worked as a night security guard at a fancy lodging facility.

I was dumbfounded. I was caught in a strange position with this man and his wife. But it wasn't my trouble; it was theirs. I hadn't done anything out of line.

"I tried calling you and you didn't answer your phone like you never do. So, I decided to get off work early and take the liberty to come and look for you. Since I know you like to go out all the time, I figured I'd start here and look for your car."

I remained quiet, listening to their quickly escalating conversation. For some reason, I found it all amusing. It was like something out of the scene of a movie. I couldn't believe she walked around downtown till she found his car, as if she was sure to find it in this area.

"Are you going to answer my question, Brandon? Who is your friend that you're secretly partying with when you should be at home with your children?"

"Secretly partying with? There's nothing a secret about her. That's Keisha. The same one you talked to over the phone. The same woman whose phone you'd call whenever you feel the need to. What's your problem? Are you playing spy detective on me now?" Brandon rattled off. "I don't have anything to hide. You were the one that told me to go find friends. To just get out of your face and leave you alone. Now that I've done what you've asked, you have a problem with that. I don't go snooping around trying to find out about you and your little friend. So why do you feel the need to do all of this?"

Right in front of me, they turned it into a full-blown argument. All of thirty minutes they went back and forth. Most of the cars were now gone, and I wanted to go home. It was none of my business and I didn't care.

"Um, I'm not trying to be rude, but Brandon, can you take me home?"

At that, they quieted down. He took me home and I didn't hear from him till the next day. When he got off work he showed up at my place. He told me that night they continued arguing until the crack of dawn. He was given an ultimatum to choose between me, his friend, and her, his wife. He said he made the choice to leave because it wasn't right that she was trying to control his life. She demanded that he got rid of his female friends while she held on to her male friends. He refused to let her dominate and control him. Then she countered, saying he didn't have to get rid of all his friends, just me, because she didn't trust how I looked.

I giggled to myself. Surely, he didn't believe that was her reason for disliking me. I wasn't married to her, he was. And he was the one she needed to worry about. Not me. But as his friend, I continued to lend a listening ear as he vented.

He began to share with me all the troubles in their marriage. She had cheated on him with a male friend she refused to let go of. Before she was found out, she left him in the house for nearly three weeks to care for his children alone, during which time Brandon had no idea of her whereabouts until his friend showed him where his other car was. He went there and waited outside of the house, her lover's place, for the perfect moment to confront her. When they came face to face, she told Brandon she never loved him and didn't know why she married him. If she could, she said, she'd leave and never come back. Crushed, Brandon left her with her lover.

Now I understood why he refused to let go of me, a close friend. I also understood why he spent so much time away from home. I felt sorry for him. He didn't deserve that treatment. "You could stay here for a few days if you wanted," I said, "if you can't go home now and don't have somewhere else to crash." He accepted without hesitation. The day after, he began moving his things into my place.

The following Sunday, I invited him to go to church with me. I was introduced to a church by a young lady I called my God sister and had already gone once. The pastor there was a prophet, more real and street than any preacher I'd ever seen. I could relate to his sermons, and he seemed to relate to those of us who had it rough and needed solid guidance. Brandon didn't have anything else planned, so he went with me.

It was my second time attending a Sunday service at that church, and Brandon's first. While the service was ending in prayer, the pastor paused. Pointing in Brandon's direction, he said, "The new dude, I need you to come up front. I got a word for you from the Lord."

Everybody was quiet. You could've heard a pin drop. A couple of new visitors looked at each other, unsure if the pastor was referring to them.

"No, the new guy sitting beside the new young lady," the pastor spoke again. "As a matter of fact, I need you both to come here."

Now there was no doubt who he was speaking to. Brandon and I got up and walked up to the front of the assembly. Everyone watched in silence.

FINDING AND RIPPING OUT THE ROOTS OF UGLINESS

The pastor smiled when Brandon got to the front and stood before him. After introducing himself and asking Brandon his name, the pastor began prophesying. "God said that the situation that you're going through is over. He has freed you from the yoke of bondage. You already know what I'm talking about; I don't need to say anymore." Turning to me, the pastor said, "God said that the husband you been praying for, that's him. You've been faithfully asking the Lord for your husband, right? Well, he's been right in your face the whole time."

Hearing his words, I covered my trembling lips with both my hands as tears began to gather in my eyes. I had only been to this church for the second time and never even spoken with this pastor. We were practically strangers, but he knew I had been asking God for a husband! There was no way he could've known unless God had revealed it to him.

He turned back to Brandon again. "Man, God gave you a full-blown hustler. I don't even know if you know what to do with her," he said with a hearty laughter.

What a revelation! The man I had been close friends with turned out to be the man God saw fit for me. That changed everything. I now felt free to develop a deeper, more intimate relationship with Brandon.

He began his divorce proceedings, and I did everything to support him in his work, in his transition out of that marriage, in building our future together.

One year later, we were living in a place of our own and my two boys joined us. Within days after his divorce was final, we exchanged vows before the justice of the peace. I was pregnant, and only four months later I gave birth to my beautiful baby girl.

Although everything was turning out beautifully, something in the back of my mind always bugged me. How could God have found favor in my dating a married man? God honors marriages, and if Brandon was truly the man for me, why didn't that pastor tell us we needed to wait until the time was right—until he was no longer married to another woman—to begin our relationship? I wondered at times if God honored the marriage vow we exchanged since we were together before he was officially divorced.

Regardless of this quiet nagging voice, I carried on living my life. For the most part, I believed what we did was fine. After all, we were encouraged by a man of God, who couldn't have known about my secret prayers if it weren't for God's direct revelation.

However, as I grew more mature in my faith, I became more and more sure that I had done a terrible wrong to Brandon's first family. I was at least an accomplice in wrecking his marriage, although it already had profound issues before I came into the picture. The preacher's words were no excuse for our actions. Human beings make mistakes, although God never does. I should have known better not to take a mere mortal's words and run with it. I should have acted according to the eternal word of God—honor marriages.

In my ignorance of what pleased God, I became an adulterer who would reap the consequences of my actions. It didn't take long for me to see the true colors of the man I wrongfully married. Through all his charming and deceptive laughter, he was a liar. He was dishonest with me just as he was with his first wife.

I felt foolish yet again. Not only had I ended up in a lie I had no business in, it was something I never wanted. Brandon was somewhat attractive, but by far was he my taste. There were enough about him that bothered me that I didn't feel in love with him. I began learning how to love him. Had it not been for that pastor, we never would've happened. Before that Sunday, all I ever really wanted was to be friends with Brandon. On top of my own misery, I knew I was at least one of the causes that broke up his first marriage.

However unhappy I was, the reality was I *was* married. I remembered how older people used to say that all marriages had their ups and downs, and as long as you didn't go to bed mad at each other and continued to work on it, things would improve. I tried that. It didn't work. Even if I went to bed with full forgiveness and acceptance of Brandon's lies and mistreatment of me, when I woke up I'd see the same person. The more I tried to make our marriage work, the more I began to hate him.

Realizing that I couldn't change Brandon, I looked within to see what I could do to make our life easier. It was then that I discovered that I had deep-rooted problems. I was always yearning for something more, always searching but never satisfied. Could it be because I needed education, which would give me a more secure job and more promising future?

I went back to school and earned my general education diploma. From there, I immediately enrolled in college, where I studied business management. That wasn't the answer. I still found myself discontent, restless in a nine-to-five job. Somewhere deep within, I knew my life was more than that. So, I continued to search for what it was that I needed.

It occurred to me that I enjoyed hustling, which was much more challenging than the regular management job and demanded much more focus and creativity. That felt good to me however, and I wanted to go back to that, although not in the same industry. Being disheartened by Brandon's dishonesty and betrayals, I went with one of the first ideas that came to me that could begin to free myself from the distractions and sorrows of my marriage—I became a promoter of exotic dancers. I struggled between the intense desire to honor God and the suffocation that living with Brandon gave me. I wanted out of the misery of my marriage, and quickly I chose to hustle in whatever trade I could do so legally, in hopes that I'd find immediate relief from my unhappiness.

Having set my mind on trying hustling again, but as a promoter, I posted ads looking for potential dolls. Within a day, more than a handful applied. I interviewed them and asked them to demonstrate their skills. I needed to see they were as serious as I was about earning money, so just the average stripper wouldn't have cut it. I was looking for entertainers easy on the eyes, attractive in her seduction, and able to put on a great performance. The ideal candidate would know how to move her body to entice men to come out of their pockets. I knew the power of sex and that harnessing that industry could bring in tons of cash for me.

I had some success right away, and intended to travel from state to state with my entourage of dolls. I was a pimp, in a sense, of being the go-to woman for naked erotic strippers. If there was a bachelor or bachelorette party that needed strippers, I was there. I found myself bringing the latest, most requested porn stars to Richmond. I even secured girls from World Star Hip Hop to perform in night clubs. I became known in the industry as "Lady K," and I fell in love with the entertainment industry. As I expanded my gig, I planned to spread my wings even wider.

Back at home, there was never-ending confusion with Brandon. He wasted no time in finding someone to cheat on me with. It might or might not have been full-blown betrayal involving sexual intercourse, but infidelity takes many forms, not just physical union. I believe that whatever you did in the absence of your spouse that you wouldn't do in their presence is cheating. If that thing causes you to be sneaky and deceitful, you know it's wrong.

Perhaps his addiction to porn led to a habit of sneaky behavior, or maybe he was simply a habitual liar. Whatever the case, his emotional affairs never ended, and that amongst other things made him my enemy. Not only did he cheat on me, he didn't support my hustle and didn't understand why investing in anything was necessary. While I worked hard to make money, he badmouthed about me to his family and friends and turned many of them against me.

Finally, I told him our time would soon come to an end. I had learned to love him, but he abused my love. He didn't give me even the minimal respect I deserved as a human being—no one deserved to be lied to—let alone the respect I deserved as his wife. I couldn't tolerate his disloyalty any longer, and I told him I wanted out.

He tried to convince to stay for the sake of our daughter. But that made me want out even more. Why would any mother want her child to grow up with a cheat who couldn't manage to tell a straight truth? Or witness constant bickering back and forth.

Even as I made plans to leave Brandon behind, I didn't blame him for everything that went wrong in our marriage. I was conscious of the possibility that I also contributed to our issues. Although I couldn't identify the root of my problems yet, or even put my finger on what my problems were, I knew with the kind of past I lived, there was bound to be baggage. The kind of trauma and lifestyle that left its mark.

As I continued in my self-discovery, I was firm in my decision to end it all with Brandon. There was no doubt that he and I were wrongfully married. The last straw was when his ex-wife told me they had an affair when I was pregnant with my daughter, and Brandon probably fathered her last child. I had no words to describe or explain his betrayal. All I knew was there was no reason to delay things. I decided to find a place to live behind his back.

Brandon beat me to the punch and stopped coming home. He simply upped and left for his new family, where he thought grass was greener and more plentiful. Unknowingly, he waited for my daughter's school bus to deliver her home and he took her without my permission. Even withdrawing her from her school and keeping her away from me.

It was good riddance for me. He was out of my hair and into the woman who wanted him. All the better. Now I could take care of business without having to argue with him or explain anything to him. As soon as I signed the lease for the new apartment, I filed for divorce. He was now stuck with his new grass.

While I was happy that he was gone, I was torn to pieces over my daughter. The reality was that it was karma having her vengeance at me. I went through exactly what I made Brandon's first wife go through. I took her husband, and now someone else came to take my husband. Had I truly been a godly woman, I would've known it was immoral to get involved with Brandon while he was still married. But now I knew, and I would never make the same mistake again.

Shortly after I filed for divorce, I found myself in and out of court. There was always some kind of dispute, because in Brandon's and his new partner's hostility, they wanted badly to see me fail. Suddenly, Brandon was questioning the paternity of my daughter, which was never an issue before. It was as annoying for me as it was laughable. I let Brandon and his girlfriend do their circus act and warned him I wasn't playing along.

Since I didn't play their game, they couldn't make the noise for long. Our divorce was finalized more quickly than expected. His infidelity set me free from the bond of marriage. But I knew there were deeper problems in both of us that we couldn't even see at the time. In any event, I was relieved that the marriage was dissolved; it wasn't one that honored God. In becoming involved with each other while Brandon was still married to his first wife, we committed adultery, trampling on God's law as if His words didn't matter. That blatant disobedience quickly reaped its ugly reward, and I had learned my lesson.

I had a new relationship, with an old fling I'd met years ago, long before Brandon. This time it lasted two short years, and I found myself in a place of unhappiness again. It wasn't infidelity this time, but the familiar demons that rode my partner's back. I didn't know about his past drug use until we were into our relationship already.

In the beginning, he was able to put those monsters under subjection by relying heavily on the popular Narcotics Anonymous meetings, where addicts or ex-addicts convinced one another that they all had a disease that they were stuck with for life. Only constant meetings would keep them clean and sober. My partner preferred the truth of man over the Power of God, and as I knew it would happen, he never got rid of his demons.

His relapse affected me in the worst way. I found myself on an emotional roller-coaster. I was miserable because one after another, men came into my life and exerted such an influence on how I lived and thought and felt. I asked God to enlighten me and bless me with the determination to allow only Him the power to determine my happiness. My happiness should only be in the hands of my Lord, not Brandon, not my new boyfriend, not anyone else. The Lord already said we are to have no other gods before Him.

Not quite a year into our relationship, I started making plans to relocate. Georgia had my eye. But I didn't want to leave him, so I asked him to join me. But as soon as I asked him, I realized there was a problem. I had given him the key to my happiness, and that was where everything was wrong. I needed to rely solely on God for my happiness, but I didn't know how to.

I began talking with God more than ever before. I asked him to show me to myself and helped me recognize my troubles. I needed to be honest with God about all the hurts from my past, all the needs I had in the present. I needed to understand what my root problem was and if I had been carrying the same problems everywhere I went—because if I was, then moving to Georgia wouldn't make things better, with or without my new boyfriend.

I sought God earnestly, but the process of healing was as painful as it was protracted. God showed me where the ugly roots of my life were, one by one. When it became overwhelming, God reminded me that there could be no beautiful tree or delicious fruits from ugly, rotten roots. I had to find those roots and remove them entirely. God is the Great Gardener, and as any gardener knows, hideous weeds had to be removed before new growth could begin. He was waiting to show me the beautiful blossoms of my life if I would do the work of uprooting the weeds in my soul.

As God showed me the ugly roots, I also asked for His help in working through it all. I felt it. I felt the peace of God enveloping my being as if I were wrapped in a blanket. In that moment, I experienced a happiness deeper than anything I'd known, a solace sweeter than anything I'd tasted, and a lightness I'd never felt before. My God had become my elation.

My boyfriend began questioning my cheerfulness as if it were a strange thing or that I didn't deserve it. It became clear to me that because of his own pains, he wanted to see me in distress too. I loved him and wanted the best for him, but that love didn't mean I had to stay with him. I had to choose between staying with him and turning back on God's promises or going on the path God had shown me, which led to light and peace. The choice was clear. There was no competition with God.

I began exploring Georgia, making frequent trips between my potential new home and Richmond. I wasn't only moving my place of residence; I was also going to pursue a different path, one that held purpose and meaning. Going forward, my life would be spent serving good causes and honoring God. My boyfriend wasn't on board with me, and I understood it wasn't something anyone could force on anyone else.

Our difference was so great that even my seven-year-old daughter noticed and commented on it. That same guy she took a great liking to had become someone else in her eyes, and though she couldn't explain it, she only knew she didn't like it. I tried to rescue him out of that life multiple times, but quickly I learned and accepted that our paths were different. That sometimes people are just meant to go different ways. In the end, we parted ways peacefully.

I was ready for my new path. Here, I would not look to a man for happiness, validation, or comfort. I made up my mind that my life was in God's hands alone, and I'd live for Him alone. No one else had the power to decide how I should live and whether I could be happy. I *was* already happy, and no one could take that away from me, because my God had given me inner peace and helped me in a way that I'd never been helped.

I was ready for new growth, for beautiful blossoms, and godly fruits.

CHAPTER 17

THE OTHER SIDE OF THE STORM

It was a beautiful day in the middle of June 2016 when CeQuan and Ketwan helped their sister and I load our things onto a moving truck. The next day we were leaving Richmond for good. My daughter and I were excited; my boys were happy for me too.

At 5:00 a.m., my daughter and I headed for the highway. We stopped by 7-11 first to get breakfast and coffee. Then we continued on Highway 95. With the windows cracked and the breeze coming through, I cried, with relief and liberation.

As I cruised along, my mind played over and over the story of my life, from my earliest memories to that moment on the road. Everything, it seemed, had a consequence that caught up sooner or later. I chuckled when I remembered Brandon telling me the agony of having to live with the consequence of his betrayal of my trust. He said what looked like greener grass when he was my husband, now was nothing more than artificial turf fertilized with horse manure, because his mistress turned out to be his worst mistake in life. That guy had some sense of humor!

I had moments of brief laugh like that through the twenty some years of my life, but most of that time was consumed in one dark storm after another. I had gone down to depths of hell that I wouldn't wish on my worst enemy, yet today I stood firm on my two feet. I had made so many bad decisions and hurt so many people that I didn't think I deserved a second chance, but I was given a second chance, a third chance, and many more chances, until I was back on my feet.

It's nothing short of amazing that I'm able to share my story of troubles, hurts and deep dark secrets; how I was blessed with the gift of resilience to bounce back stronger than ever. He allowed me to go through those storms in order that I'd mature and gain wisdom, in a process that was a complete, utter transformation that was unlike anything I've ever experienced. Those life lessons weren't intended for me to hang on to hate or grudges; no, The Most High gave me those lessons to show me the depth of human depravity, the intensity of human suffering, and the hope available in Him that was just as broad, deep, and powerful as any trauma that come our way.

This girl made it. She emerged from the storm of life in one piece, not defeated, but transformed into a butterfly that reflects God's glory. From a half-abandoned little girl, to a drug-dealing teenager and young adult, unwed mother of two, cross-addicted inmate, homeless prostituting junkie, to a renewed woman. The strength she had to persevere through it all was not hers—it was a gift from above. It's only because of God's grace that today, you can not find a trace of her past on her face, however closely you examined her eyes and smile.

In my darkest moments, when I went without food or had nowhere to lay my head, God was there. When I thought I was on top of the world, dipped in the latest fashion and bringing in streams of money, God was there. When I thought I was utterly alone, God was there. If He seemed absent, it was only Him allowing me to undergo the refining fires, under His ever-watchful protection, so that I might see the severity of my situation and my radical need of my Lord. He brought me back eventually. The young girl who was once lost had been found. I who was had no idea of who the LORD is, have a clearer understanding. I was born again, and in my rebirth, I now understand the world that once seemed so confusing and dark to me.

It's a beautiful blessing to be given a pair of spiritual glasses you've never worn before. I am blessed beyond measure, not because of anything material, but because God spared me and gave me new life when I was once walking dead. He gave me the power I needed to leave the storms behind and follow Him. I was given a new mind, not just any mind, but one with purpose; capable of thinking clearly and understanding the truth. To me, that is precious above all things. God reoriented my mind toward Himself, so to Him I turned, and I no longer live in the fear of the unknown. Rather, having returned unto the Laws, Statutes and Commandments of OUR LORD, I am more confident than I've ever been about my direction. One thing is for sure; no good thing will the LORD withhold from those who love Him, and I've learned that the keeping of His commandments proves your love for him (1 John 5:3 KJV).

In Atlanta, God showed me what He had in store for me. He gave me a heart full of passion to help others, a heart that burns with the zeal of helping the weak and directing the lost—those walking in the path I once followed.

As soon as I settled my daughter and myself in our new apartment, I filed for and registered my businesses in Georgia; all lawful businesses operating with a mission to serve and support those of my people who're lost, but willing novices desiring change. No longer driven by the desire for wealth, my life has taken on a whole new meaning. I find solace in making a positive difference and being the change I speak about.

Through the storm and now on the other side of it, I have learned to listen to God's voice, His word. This is the only way to gain wisdom. I also learned that whatever wisdom I gain, it will be tested and refined by fire. That fire isn't used to consume us, only to prove us. Gold doesn't become pure until it has been refined; even the most flawless diamonds emerges from extremely pressurized conditions. Do you desire to have a life full of useful and awesome value? Surely your story has purpose behind it, just as mine does. How will you find your purpose? Being frivolous in life will not get you there. You'll only waste years of life chasing something that has no meaning. What's your life worth? An even better question; what about those who follow your example?

Never be ashamed of your struggles and troubles. Most have gone through life having to deal with some of them. Whether you've succeeded or failed in your struggles, there is always hope for the future. Never let your past failures define you, or allow someone else to make you feel unworthy because of them. As long as there is breath in you, your story is not over yet!

You are not your past, so don't be enslaved to the stigma of labels. The past is simply that—the *past*. And no one with true wisdom lives for yesterday, for our God is forgiving and compassionate toward His people. Forgive yourself, repent and come back to His laws, and draw closer to Him. Under His umbrella of protection, you will experience a transformation that will make you unrecognizable. Only then can His glory shine through you, and only then will you be able to walk in the purpose He has given to your life.

Today, I come into the lives of law-breakers and show them how they might live as law-abiding citizens. I help them unlearn their former ways of thinking and empower them to embrace the change that awaits them. I help give a voice of reason where there is no voice, I am a mother to the motherless, and I help recidivists develop solutions who formerly saw no way of escape from the criminal life that held them captive.

This is my story, my transformation, and my hope is that you will experience one too if you haven't.

My heart goes out to you. I love you though I've yet to meet you. If you are going through a hard time or are recovering from one, I understand your pain and frustration. I know exactly what it feels like. I pray that God gives you the strength to bare it, the grace to weather your storm, and the wisdom to make it through. Hang in there, chin up, and have hope—for through the storm there is a rainbow.

A Final Prayer
Dear God, I thank you for my life. But what is it without you? I thank you for the grace and mercy you've kept me covered with. I thank you for the lives of those reading this book. I pray that in some way you'll touch those hearts and give them understanding, understanding of why they struggle. You said your sheep know your voice, but strangers will not follow. Bless your sheep with ears to hear and eyes to see. For our people are so lost; they claim they know you yet their hearts are far from you. Merciful God, allow your sheep to hear your voice and to seek your face like never before. For I understand that your voice is your word; give them understanding Father. Give them a hunger and thirst for the truth of your word like they've never known before; to understand that we must return unto you with repented hearts, willing to depart from the error of our ways and keep your laws dear Father.

I thank you for this beautiful testimony you've crafted in my life.

Through the storm, your light shines through, and may your people receive healing from this testimony. Please break them loose from the bondage that keeps them captive, and set them free. I love them the way you said we should love. I desire that even they put away the hate for our brethren and love also; for if we see Christ in one another, there would be no hate.

I am of service to you, dear Lord. I am honored to walk in honor of you, and to have walked the path that I've walked. For 'Through the Storm' I've gained wisdom that comes with experience, which allows me to be a mother to the motherless, a voice for the lost, and a woman of understanding. I thank you and I love you with my heart, soul and strength. I thank you for being my one and only God, my Father. I thank you for never giving up on me even when I deserted you, when I turned my back on you thinking some man could love me better than you can. I'm so sorry for the ways I've ever hurt you. I repent of all my sins; the transgression of your law. Please forgive my rebellion. I thank you so much for setting me free. I can breathe now because you have become the fresh breath my lungs need. I feel so protected and covered by your hedge of protection. My heart is forever grateful and thankful to you Father!

Again, I thank you, and I ask all these things in the name of my Lord and Savior, Jesus the Christ. Amen.

The law of the LORD is perfect, converting the soul; the testimony of the LORD is sure, making wise the simple.
— Psalm 19:7

EPILOGUE

Everyone that appears in my story has been given fictitious names, but each one was a real person in my life. Some of them have continued on their same paths after I parted ways with them, and others have made changes.

Today, Ms. Jay is doing well, clean for six to seven years now.

Biggs is married and has given me my only beautiful niece and nephew. He hasn't found what he feels is the true answer he has been searching for all these years—why did Mom leave him with Sister but brought me with her? He would have loved to have closure to this and other questions, but even with the unanswered questions, Biggs and I love each other and have remained close, despite the physical distance between us.

Sister, my dear great-grandmother, passed when CeQuan was only five months old. With her death, what used to be a tightly knit family fell apart and we just couldn't pull it back together.

Mr. Pete has been clean for some time now. Jasmine and Bella are both mothers and enjoying their children. We haven't kept in touch, but I still consider them my dear sisters to this day.

Jay married his cheat and has stayed married to her for quite some time now.

Lil T passed a few years back. Jeanette relocated to North Carolina with her only child and is doing well. The last I heard of Sonja was that she literally lost her mind, a total different person. Marcus still battles his drug use today, and Maurice, my brother always, is married with a house full of children. Allison, my nosey neighbor, has been clean for ten years or more and is doing great. Mandy, from what I hear, appears to

EPILOGUE

be doing well. I haven't seen Cuban since I stopped buying product from him in the 90s. My cousin Craig is a married family man, presumed to be doing well.

Brandon has parted ways from his mistress/girlfriend and remains active in his daughter's life.

My dad and I never built a relationship, and I've only seen him once in Virginia after I took his van and left DC. It's as if we never really reunited. The boyfriend whom I was so fund of, now resides in New York and is presumed to be doing well.

Last but certainly not least, my boys are now twenty-four and twenty-one, both high school graduates. They reside in Virginia with plans of joining me in Georgia in the near future. They each have given me one grandchild and both are great dads. My lovely grandchildren are still toddlers, and the fact that I'm a grandmother still hasn't quite sunk in yet.

ABOUT THE AUTHOR

Formerly known as Lakeisha McQuinn, Amina I. is a mentor, business owner, and first-time author. Having endured the experiences described in *Through the Storm* and learned from them, she was inspired to create a nonprofit organization, A New Beginning, Inc., serving convicted men and women who are soon to be released, as well as those who have already paid their debts to society and are actively seeking change but need assistance of various kinds. The organization is dedicated to motivating and uplifting those who've felt all hope is lost, but are willing to embrace change with the support of A New Beginning. Amina's days are spent traveling to jails and prison houses, where she gives public speeches and coaches inmates to prepare them for new life on the other side of the prison walls.

Amina has also created her own fashion powerhouse, AminaI., offering a line of refined clothing to the virtuous woman who takes pride in her nationality. The line has clothing for every occasion, from the nine-to-five environment and the everyday look, to the date night on the town with the husband, and tailor-made garments designed for a special event. Whatever the occasion, AminaI. has the attire for you that reflects your inner beauty—beautiful, elegant, humble, spirited woman of God, to be respected.

Amina can also be found on social media, where she mentors women on virtue, life, health, and beauty. She's also the creator of MFB Entertainment, with which she travels and promotes the gospel through music. Be on the lookout—she and her crew may be coming to a venue near you.

www.ingramcontent.com/pod-product-compliance
Lightning Source LLC
Chambersburg PA
CBHW031313150426
43191CB00005B/203